Some
of My Best
Friends are
Fishermen

Some of My Best Friends are Fishermen

John Craig

McClelland & Stewart Limited

Copyright © 1976 McClelland and Stewart Limited

ALL RIGHTS RESERVED

ISBN:0-7710-2308-1

The Canadian Publishers
McClelland and Stewart Limited
25 Hollinger Road
Toronto, Ontario

Printed and bound in Canada

Contents

Foreword

I've been a fisherman for as long as I can remember. I say that neither apologetically, nor with any particular pride; it was just something that happened, like having flat feet or being able to crack your knuckles.

I suppose my mother was mainly responsible. She loved to stillfish for bass from the old, white skiff we had, and it was from her that I received my earliest education in the Art of Fishing. Piscatorial 101A. My dad occasionally dragged a trolling spoon behing his canoe, but I never remember him catching anything, and I doubt that he really wanted to: F.D.C. was always more of a philosopher than an activist, and the reality of catching, clubbing, and cleaning a muskie would have infringed upon the aesthetic charms of paddling along a shoreline on an August morning — far enough out to be safe from all but the most wanderlusting 'lunge — and *thinking about* the monsters that lurked in the weed beds and along the shoals.

Those early summers were spent at Stoney Lake in Ontario's Kawarthas. Since then I've fished in many parts of Canada — from Newfoundland to Manitoba, and from the American border to the southern fringes of the tundra, and have established more than a nodding acquaintance with most of the denizens of the eastern Canadian depths — from muskies to mudcats, from walleyes to whitefish, from largemouths to ling, from twenty-five pound Great Northerns to the skinny little pike the natives call "jackfish", from speckled trout to rainbows to browns to lake trout, from smallmouths to sunfish to smelts.

I've had a lot of fun fishing, and it seems appropriate to share some of the good times with my fellow addicts, other incurables who, like me, know that they will never kick the habit. Maybe this book will help to fill in a couple of those long, cold winter nights when it is still a couple of months too early to start thinking about mending your waders and oiling your favourite reel for another season.

I do not agree with those sho say that you have to be crazy to be a fisherman. It can, however, be a real asset since, once you are certifiably bananas about fishing, you no longer have to try to explain your suspect behaviour — such as why you insist on standing in the middle of some swollen stream, with cakes of ice bobbing past you, and icy water lapping over the tops of your waders, in the Antarctic, predawn chill on the opening day of trout season. Or the logic of sitting in a metal boat, with the rain trickling down the back of your neck and chain-lightning flashing all around, in the conviction that, since you haven't had so much as a nibble for two hours, the bass are overdue to start hitting — when you could be reclining in front of a crackling fire, with a very dry martini in your hand, watching the Reds and Dodgers on television.

Anyway, crazy or not, show me a guy who likes to fish, and I'll show you somebody who can't be all bad. I don't know that I'd like my daughter to marry one, but some of my best friends are fishermen.

This book is for them.

1.
One of Our Buses Is Missing

When I was a kid, growing up in Peterborough, Ontario, in the thirties, fishing was practically a way of life. As much as we loved hockey, it was really just a way to help get from the close of muskie season at the end of October to the opening of trout season at the beginning of May.

True, the Great Depression placed severe restrictions on travel, and we couldn't go too far afield to find the big ones, but it gave the unemployed a lot more time to get lines into the water. Also, for those who needed an excuse to escape a nagging wife, it could be persuasively argued that angling was one of the few legal ways left, short of working for a living, to put some food on the table.

Fortunately, there was respectable fishing within the city limits — in the Otonabee River, which cut through the middle of town, and the modest swelling of it, which is called Little Lake, towards the south end. I remember one spring of particularly high water when the pickerel were spawning near second base in the local ball field, and the odd good fish was caught (or speared) while trying to stretch a single into a double.

Men used to sit up all night at the London Street dam to haul a couple of writhing eels from the roiling currents of the raceway, then walk stiffly home along the deserted streets of the early morning with the evening meal wrapped in a burlap sack.

You could catch bass almost anywhere along the river, although they didn't run to much size, and you could take just about all the sunfish and perch you wanted on a bent pin and a worm.

There was a perennial rumour going around then that voracious, shark-like muskies lurked near the packing house plant on Little Lake, feeding on the scraps of meat that presumably were thrown into the water from the cutting floor. If so, nobody ever caught one, as far as I know, although the story effectively prevented us from swimming in that immediate vicinity.

There were some quite respectable, non-meat-eating 'lunge in the small lake though, and the local Chamber of Commerce was not open to a charge of apocrypha when it boasted that fifteen to twenty-pound catches were taken each summer "within sight of the town clock", atop the red tower at the foot of the main street.

The opening of the pickerel season, about the middle of May , was one of the highlights of the year, in terms of community enthusiasm and participation easily outstripping such other annual events as the district hockey playoffs, the fall fair, and the Orangemen's parade on the twelfth of July. Opening "day" always took place at midnight on the Friday closest to the middle of the month, and most of the action was to be found below the dam at the south end of town.

Around eleven o'clock on that long-awaited night, people would begin to gather from all parts of the city — solitary men, youths with their girlfriends, whole families including babies in carriages, and septuagenarians happy to be there to greet another spring. If it was a chilly night, some would build bonfires along the bank. Whatever the circumstances, the opening-nighters brought with them an astonishing variety of equipment and accessories — garden chairs, tents, portable stoves, blankets, flashlights, picnic lunch hampers, packs of cards, thermos bottles, teething rings for the very young, and chamber pots for the very old. A nearby snack-bar did as much business on that one night as in any ten-day period throughout the rest of the year.

As midnight drew near, everybody would begin to move down towards the river — a trickle at first, swelling to a floodtide as the countdown continued. There would be several hundred anglers, lining both banks and clinging precariously to every possible foothold on the dam itself. Tackle boxes would be opened, lures selected and snapped onto leaders. Worm cans were at hand, the lids of minnow buckets open. Tense impatience reigned. At last six months of winter could be put into the past.

"What time you got?"

"Bout three minutes to go, I make it."

There was always at least one who cheated a little, like a sprinter getting a jump off the blocks. Somewhere off in the darkness the whir of a casting reel would be heard, and then everyone would spring into action. Hundreds of rod-tips whipped back, hundreds of lures flew out into the night. Among all of those first-of-the-year casts, perhaps because of chilled fingers or over-eagerness or un-oiled reels or the long winter lay-off, there were bound to be quite a few back-lashes. These unfortunates struggled to unravel their birds' nests in the darkness, while their stripped lines formed ragged loops across the fast current. Many lures would sink and get snagged on bottom. Inevitably others would get caught up on underwater obstructions, and by 12:05 the rapids below the dam would be one gigantic, hopelessly tangled cat's cradle, and half the fishermen would be out of action.

As a friend of mine said, more walleyes probably laughed themselves to death than were caught on those opening nights. But any kind of fishing was better than no fishing at all.

The real spirit of the time was probably best captured in an incident involving one of the town's bus drivers. There were five public transportation routes in the little city, and the buses used to meet every half-hour at an intersection on the main street, a block from the town clock.

One of those routes was called the Byersville run, and it covered the southern part of the city, including a deserted stretch of road along the river. The regular driver on that circuit was a man we shall call 'Hap'. He was a short, stocky guy, probably around thirty-five, who always wore pant clips around the cuffs of his trousers, although I never remember seeing him on a bicycle; maybe he had owned one before the onset of the Depression, and wore them as a reminder that there had once been a time when he could afford to buy tires for it. Hap was an easy-going, quiet man, with a restrained but keen sense of humour that let him roll with a lot of punches; the kind of friend that you always enjoy being with, even if you only see him occasionally. He and I used to fish together quite often in Little Lake, casting out of an old green canoe his father-in-law kept beside one of the boathouses south of the railway bridge. Hap had four or five kids, and lived in a rented house in a terrace in the south part of town. He played third base on one of the city league softball teams and was a reliable fielder, even though he never hit anywhere near his roly-poly weight, about two-forty.

Hap was lucky, of course, to have a steady job of any kind in those years, and particularly fortunate to draw the Byersville route, which accounted for relatively few passengers and was only maintained as a political sop to the voters in that part of town. It was hardly used after dark, and when he had the night shift Hap could easily pick up five or six minutes on the southern leg of his circuit. He had developed the habit of parking his bus beside the road, hopping out with the casting rod that he always kept behind the driver's seat, and taking a few casts into the river before continuing his run. Regular patrons had long accepted this, and thought nothing of being driven uptown with a couple of pickerel flopping around on the floor near the front of the bus. It was understood that each man had to feed his family the best way he could.

But one August night about ten o'clock Hap failed to show up at the rendezvous point on the main street. The drivers of the other buses waited as long as they thought they could, then one put in a call to the dispatcher to inform him of the situation before departing on their rounds — without their man in Byersville.

The dispatcher, an older man of considerable wisdom (who also liked to fish), knew where to look for Hap. He drove down and found the missing bus, parked in the usual spot beside the river. The half-dozen passengers were down on the river bank, cheering their driver on. There was a fine summer rain falling, so that the scattered lights from across the river made ragged patterns on the surface of the slow-moving current. That particular night Hap had hooked, not a routine two or three-pound pickerel, but a gargantuan muskie of the kind that the great majority of fishermen only encounter in their dreams.

The dispatcher joined the passengers in offering advice and encouragement. It evolved into an epic struggle. Again and again Hap brought the monster in to the shallows under the gravelly bank, but each time, just when he seemed ready to expire, Mr. Muskie would be off again, dancing across, and leaping over, the rain-flecked surface of the river. The big fish finally began to show signs of tiring the eighth or ninth time he was coaxed in near shore.

"Keep him coming, Hap," the dispatcher shouted. "Don't give him any slack."

"You don't give this fish anything," Hap said. "He takes what he wants."

"How are you gonna get him up the bank?"

"I don't know."

"Damn."

The dispatcher waited a couple more minutes, then could restrain himself no longer. Hopping around on first one leg and then the other, he took off his shoes and socks and rolled up his pant legs.

"What are you going to do?" Hap asked.

"I'll haul him out for you" the dispatcher said, wading out into the night-enveloped water. The bottom shelved off gradually but there was considerable current at that point in the river, and the dispatcher almost lost his footing a couple of times. Then there was a lot of threshing around out in the water, and considerable swearing. Neither Hap nor any of the onlookers could tell what was going on, but finally the dispatcher came wading back up onto the shore, the huge, slippery, and still far from subdued muskie cradled in his arms. He waddled a few steps and laid the fish down in the bus' headlights, and Hap and the others crowded around to admire the catch. It was subsequently weighed at a shade over thirty pounds on the scales at Beuhler's Butcher Shoppe ("We Never Close As Long As There's A Customer To Be Served") a block north of the dam. One of the best 'lunge caught in our area that summer, Hap's was.

The dispatcher in his official report subsequently explained the episode in terms of a partial failure in the steering system of the Byersville bus, and Hap received a written commendation from the Chairman of the local Transit Authority for his prudence in protecting the safety of his passengers. He could, of course, just as easily have been fired, a terrifying prospect for a man with a wife and several kids in those difficult times. In the days that followed somebody asked Hap if he hadn't been worried about that eventuality.

"Damn right," Hap replied, "but I figured I didn't have any choice."

"You could have cut the line," another man pointed out.

Hap just stared at him, his tightly crimped, black eyebrows attesting to his puzzlement.

"What ?" he asked finally.

"Well, it's just that a job's a job, in these times and all" the other man added by way of clarification.

Hap thought about that the way a man does when a question merits serious contemplation, then nodded slowly.

"Yep" he said, "we surely coulda wound up on the dole, me and the missus and the whole shebang."

"So why not let it go ?."

Hap paused, thinking deeply, while he carefully formulated his answer.

"Well, see, I was pretty sure I wouldn't be able to find another job, but you really can't tell about a thing like that. On the other hand I *knew* I wasn't ever gonna tie into a fish like that again. A matter of priorities, I guess you could call it."

"Way to go, Hap," somebody applauded.

And, if you're a fisherman, you will understand that my friend, Hap, had only done what he had to do.

2.
The 6:21 to Manvers

I probably would never have discovered the greatest fishing bargain of all time if I hadn't skipped school one morning when I was fifteen. It was one of those late April days when the sun is hot and the snow is gone and the grass is beginning to look green here and there, especially on the south side of buildings, and it suddenly became crystal-clear to me that a long, leisurely walk beside the river was a much more attractive possibility than sitting through Latin and algebra classes — especially since I didn't have my homework done for either one.

Just north of the railway bridge, on the far side of the river, was located what, in those Depression years, used to be called 'the hobo jungle.' Every city had one during the Thirties. It was a place where the men riding the rods could camp, reasonably free from harrassment by local police and railroad bulls; a place to rest and sleep, and cook your food if you had any, and take a bath in the river and maybe wash your clothes, and exchange rumors and gossip with others sharing the same road from Nothingford to Lost Junction and back again. Sometimes the transitory citizens would throw up rude tents or shacks, employing whatever jetsam might come to hand — packing crates, cardboard boxes, discarded pieces of fabric, railway ties, branches, anything that could be used to construct some sort of walls and a roof. There would always be a fire or two burning, and some-body would be boiling tea or heating a can of beans or toasting some stale bread or half-cooking a stolen chicken on a green stick over the flames.

A lot of the local people felt uneasy about the denizens of the hobo jungle, believing them to be a collection of escaped murderers or, worse still, Communists; but I had been there before and knew that they were just ordinary men, some good and some bad, some interesting and some dull, some generous and some conniving, who had decided that it was better to move on than to wait for something that would never happen. Less than ten years later, men just like them would constitute the First Division that sailed for France.

When I wandered into the hobo jungle that April morning I encountered a man known as 'Muskoka Red.' When I came upon him, he was making soup out of catsup, hot water, and the good parts of some onions he'd picked up behind a restaurant coming through town. He invited me to share his meal, so I sat down and we talked for an hour or more.

Muskoka Red was probably around forty years of age, a tall, angular man, almost gaunt, his thin face unshaven, with slightly stooped shoulders and the rolling, somewhat bowlegged walk of a cowpoke. It turned out, though, that he'd never had much to do with cattle; instead he'd owned a small hunting and fishing lodge up on the French River, a place he'd built himself with the help of his wife and a couple of Indians. Before that he'd worked as a section hand on the railway. The lodge had been doing allright, too — he credited a lot of their success to the fact that his wife was a great cook — until the Depression came along.

"We were in the black for the '29 season," he told me. "Had a profit for the first time, that year. Building up a regular clientele, people that liked our place and came back. Three years later she was all gone. Couldn't keep up the taxes, and the mortgage company took her over."

He had looked for work all over the north — in the mines, the lumber camps, everywhere — and then he had taken to the open road, hoping like so many others that things would somehow be better somewhere else, if a man just kept on moving long enough. Since then he had been back and forth across the country several times, and claimed to know "every foot of railroad track from one coast of the other." He was the only hobo I ever ran across who carried a supply of books with him on his travels.

"Only one thing better than reading," he said.

"What's that?" I asked

"Fishin'," he said.

The soup was ready by then, and he poured some of it from the blackened jam tin into a couple of tin mugs he took from his knapsack.

We talked about fishing for quite a while after that. Muskoka Red said that it was one of the things he missed most. Had lots of time for it, he said, but there was just no easy way a man could pack a rod along with him on the road. I suppose that losing the lodge had kind of spoiled it for him.

"Sometimes you pass a lake, though, one of those lonely lakes away up north in the wilderness, and you just know there's got to be big pike in there, or 'lunge, or bass that never have seen a hook. You surely do."

He shook his head sadly, then drank some more of his soup.

"Matter of fact" he said, "I saw a stretch of stream this morning — oh, my, that was some good looking trout water."

"Whereabouts did you see it?" I asked him.

He had come in an hour or two before on a freight out of Toronto.

"Back a few miles," he said. "Close to a flag stop. Don't recollect the name off-hand. Wait a bit, maybe this'll refresh my memory."

He took a much-handled railway timetable from his hip pocket and ran his thumb down the list of stations.

"Yep, here she is — place called Manvers," he said after a minute.

"You figure there's trout in there, eh?" I asked.

"Sure as there's water," he said.

Something about the way he expressed it made me want to test out his theory, and a couple of days later I went down to the station and picked up a schedule of my own. Peterborough was on the main CPR line from Ottawa to Toronto, and every morning at 6:21 a westbound train paused briefly in our little town on its way from the national to the provincial capital. It was only a twenty-mile trip and the station agent told me that the return fare was thirty cents. He had to look it up because he said he didn't sell tickets to Manvers very often.

Even in the depth of the Depression, it was sometimes possible to find thirty cents. You could put in a day caddying at the golf club. Or collect pop bottles, good for a 2¢ return. Or pick dew worms for twenty-five cents a hundred. Or go for fish and chips for 'Horses' Griffen, the local bookie. Or find a pinball game with an automatic pay-out that you could beat for a few nickles by manipulating a piece of wire through a crack in the glass.

I made that trip to Manvers many times over the next few summers, and the routine was always pretty much the same.

The evening before I'd dig a soup can full of worms in the vegetable garden at the back of the yard. Later on I'd pack a lunch, making sandwiches, throwing in a banana, a tomato, some homemade pickles a slice of cake, a piece of pie — the best a Depression-era kitchen could provide. This, together with the worms, my rod, a flat pipe tobacco tin which held my spare tackle, and my well-thumbed copy of the railroad timetable, would be in the front hall close to the door.

At the height of summer it would already be light when the Big Ben alarm clock went off in my room on the second floor of the big, old house — a delicious, very special time when the new day was awake, but most of the little city still slept.

Moving very stealthily, so as not to wake my parents, I'd make some breakfast in the spacious, old-fashioned kitchen. Then out the door with my gear, along the short block under the old maples and chestnut trees between the church and the library, and down the main street to the railroad station. Even at that hour, one or two merchants would be on the job, sweeping the sidewalk in front of their establishments, or setting out sale merchandise; you had to get up pretty early to make a buck during the Thirties. Apart from them, though, and perhaps a yawning policeman on the night beat, the main street would be strangely deserted in the early morning sunshine.

I'd buy my ticket from the sleepy agent, then walk along the wooden platform and listen for the train. You'd hear her first when she whistled for the railway bridge over the river. She was almost always on time. Pretty soon you'd see the headlight, still on from the night run, then hear the bell and see the steam, and the ties would bounce up and down as she pulled into the station.

A lot of the passengers in the day coaches would still be asleep at that hour of the morning, some just waking up, yawning and scratching. The Ottawa train didn't stop long in Peterborough, just time enough for the conductor to look at his pocket watch, and holler "'Board!" Then we'd be picking up speed and moving into the outskirts of the city, where you'd see a few people beginning to stir, at their back doors or in their kitchen windows, and now and then a man lucky enough to have a job setting out for work with his lunch pail.

It was a thirty-five minute ride to Manvers, a place made up of no more than a little station, a general store, and one house. You could usually find a discarded copy of an Ottawa newspaper to read on the way out. For the last mile or so before reaching Manvers the trout stream ran within sight of the train for much of the time, and it was exciting to study the pools and riffles and know that you'd be working them before the morning was out.

There were never any other passengers for Manvers, nor did I ever see anyone around the station or store. I used to wonder if anybody really lived there, or if the people had just taken up and moved on somewhere else. From where I got off I'd walk about a half-mile back along the tracks, the sound of the train having long since receded towards Toronto behind me, and nothing to disturb the dewy, early morning peace except perhaps a squawking blue jay or a chattering squirrel. The tracks ran beside a big pond that some rich men had made by damming up the stream. There was a high wire fence all around the property and sometimes the game keeper would come to the door of the club house to scrutinize me as I walked along. The pool was stocked with rainbow trout, and fortunately they had a little more trouble keeping their fish in than they did in keeping trespassers out. The speckles in the stream itself didn't run very large, but a few good sized rainbows managed to get by the dam, which added some extra excitement to the downstream fishing. When I caught one of those I didn't hurry back to replace it in the rich men's pond.

I'd pick up the stream just below the dam where a county road and a small, crumbling cement bridge crossed it. From there a stretch of four or five miles of stream sang and bubbled and lazed away in front of me, and there was good fishing all the way and not a single 'PRIVATE PROPERTY — KEEP OUT!' sign to be seen. Sometimes the stream curled back into the thick cedars, where it was shadowy and cool. In other sections it ran, sparkling in the sun, through open country.

It was a bountiful, leisurely kind of fishing. There was plenty of time, almost the whole day, and I don't recall ever seeing another angler on that stream. I used to fish with an ordinary casting rod and the same silk line I used for bass, pickerel and muskies. Most of the time I'd just tie on a small hook and bait it with a worm, occasionally trying a small spinner for added enticement. I always released any trout I caught in the early part of the day, waiting until the last hour or so before I started to keep a few for the frying pan.

Once in a while a freight train would go rumbling past, and if I was in the open at the time, I would exchange waves with the engineer, who no doubt would like to have left his hot cab and joined me. There was a place about half way along where the stream doubled tightly back on itself, forming a point of land which was almost like a miniature park, shaded at one side by a twisted and very ancient willow tree. I always ate my lunch there, sitting on a big log, drinking the cold, clear water of the stream from a tin cup. Once when I was there a hen grouse and her brood of chicks came out into the clearing, the mother paying no more attention to me than if I'd been a stump. Another time a red fox ran, panting in the mid-day heat, along the track nearby.

After lunch I would continue fishing until, about three o'clock, I came out at another station called Dranoel which, for all trivia-collectors, is Leonard, spelled backwards. From there a branch line forked off at right angles heading north to Lindsay. There was a water tower at Dranoel and occasionally I would be lucky enough to happen onto a freight train, pausing briefly on its way to Peterborough and points east. If so, and if the conductor was amiable, I might get a ride home in his caboose, thereby saving my return fare. On such occasions I would give my host a couple of the trout, and once, on a chilly day in early May, we cleaned, cooked and ate the whole string in the swaying caboose before pulling into the Peterborough freight yard.

If there was no waiting freight, I would catch the afternoon train from Toronto, in either case arriving back in Peterborough around four o'clock in the afternoon. I'd walk up the main street, now busy with the daily commerce, the trout dangling beside me to draw occasional envious glances or indignant stares.

When I got home I'd clean the fish in the summer kitchen, and we'd have them for dinner that night. Apart from the time the conductor and I ate them, I don't think I ever failed to bring back enough for the three of us. They weren't big, mostly around nine or ten inches, but those firm-fleshed, delicate-flavoured little brookies made as good eating as anybody could ever hope to come across.

All of that for thirty cents.

And, if I'd been lucky enough to hitch a ride in a caboose that day, so that I could cash in the return half of my ticket, there would still be a dime left to pay my way into the Regent Theatre to see a double-feature that evening. Plus a bag of hot Giant Redskins from Dutton's Nut Shoppe on the main street.

I never saw Muskoka Red again. I took another temporary leave of absence from school and returned to the hobo jungle a couple of days after that morning I first met him, but he had moved on — east or west, I don't know. It's silly, I suppose, to count someone as a friend just because you shared a can of catsup soup with him one morning when you skipped school more than a third of a century ago, and saw that he read books, and talked about fishing with him.

But I hope he got his lodge back, he and his wife, who was such a fabulous cook. And, if by some miracle he should read this — and he *was* a reading man, I'd want him to know that he was right about that stretch of stream beside the railway tracks near Manvers.

There were trout there, in those pools and ripples, sure enough.

3.
As Long as a Paddle!

I must have been no more than sixteen that summer, but I still remember every detail as vividly as if it had happened only an hour ago, and I was excitedly babbling out the story of what I had seen for the first time.

For most of this century my family has had a cottage on Stoney Lake, one of the Kawarthas which contribute some of the beads to the necklace of lakes and rivers which form the Trent Waterway across central Ontario.

We were able to keep it through the Depression for two reasons — the taxes were so low that my father always managed somehow to find the few dollars needed to pay them, and, because we lived a mere twenty-five miles away, we could always find some way to get there each summer, even though the family car had long since been put up on cement blocks in the garage to wait out the hard times. At least once we hitch-hiked, my mother being the first to make it, a cousin and I not checking in it until the following noon, after sleeping in a convenient, though not specifically-offered, barn.

Most of the other summer residents of Stoney Lake were well-to-do doctors, lawyers and heirs from Toronto, Buffalo, New York, Detroit, Cleveland and places like that, but we danced with their daughters to the music of the juke box in the pavilion without any display of prejudice whatsoever; they couldn't help it if they had been born into smug plenty. Hell, nobody's perfect.

It was a gentle time, a time of slender canoes and graceful skiffs, of brilliantined hair, and white flannels, of shore-dinners under the pines, and coal oil lamps sending their flickering, orange reflections across the blue-grey-black waters of the twilight and the soft summer nights. A time when it seemed six months from the end of June to the beginning of September. A time of absurdly naive innocence. Stoney Lake was a place of great muskie waters then, up to, and for a while after, World War II. American fishermen used to come by the thousands every summer from the states just south of the Great Lakes, and stay at the aging but still graceful resort hotels, in pursuit of the undisputed king of the freshwater game fish, the muskellunge.

We cottagers bought our supplies, collected our mail, and did our gossiping, courting and dancing at the hotel at Crowe's Landing, on the south shore of the lake up towards its eastern head. When you went over there in the evening, which most everybody did, part of the ritual was to inspect the day's catch brought in by the hotel guests. The guides, mostly Mississauga Indians, would lay the big fish in a row in the long, drying summer grass in front of the hotel verandah. On days when they were hitting, it would not be unusual to see eighteen or twenty muskies lying there, now and again one with its savage, prehensile jaws still opening and closing to reveal jagged rows of viciously-pointed teeth.

And these trophies would be big fish, not the kind you have to measure to see if they meet the minimum length required by the Fish & Game regulations; twenty-pounders were routine, thirty-pounders noteworthy but not exceptional. You had to get up around forty pounds before a fish would be remembered beyond the next few days, let alone into another summer.

So I had seen a lot of better-than-a-yard-long muskies by the time I reached my early 'teens, and I had caught some, too — one that went twenty-eight pounds, another a shade over thirty.

We had a St. Lawrence-style skiff in those days, a beautiful boat that resembled a broad-at-the-beam canoe, graceful and responsive and light as a feather to row, but as seaworthy as anything you would ever want to trust your life to in a sudden summer squall. I logged a lot of hours in that boat when I was a boy, collecting driftwood and pine roots for the insatiable kitchen stove, on berry-picking expeditions, exploring, just drifting in the luxuriant heat of July and August suns — and casting for muskies.

This particular evening, the one I remember most clearly from all the others, I rowed a half a mile up the lake along Caseman's Island to a place where another, smaller island forms a pocket — more like a little bay, really, than a channel, because it is almost closed off at one end by shoals, lily pads, and thick weeds. It was a fine muskie hole where I had taken a couple of decent fish the previous summer.

It was the kind of late July evening that people charged with tourist promotion try to capture with words and pictures, yet never can really catch. How can you preserve for posterity the equisite, quite undeserved luxury of watching a family of otters play along and around the trunk of a prostrated great white pine that burst from seed more than a hundred years ago? And how can you get the colours right — the black and purple reflections of the ragged trees, spindly but massed for mutual protection? The pink and orange neon lights up in the sky, giving promise for tomorrow? What can you really say about the slap of a beaver's tail? Or how describe the keening of a loon, calling for it's mate; you've been there and know about such things, or you've been somewhere else, and no piling-up of words is going to make you understand.

The sun was still an hour above the crest of the ridge along the rim of Northey's Bay, alone in the sky save for a few ragged strands of white cloud. The surface of the lake was limpid, dead calm, the boat drifting gently, not even teased by the whim of an occasional breeze. At times like that sounds carry with astonishing clarity over the water — the barking of a dog from the mainland two miles away, the closing of a screen door, an argument which continues over dirty supper dishes.

A pair of loons were calling back and forth beyond the small island; there have probably been loons there, behaving much like that, since soon after the retreat of the last Ice Age.

I was standing up in the skiff, casting with a green, white and red, jointed Pikie minnow plug, the credentials of which were already established by the teeth marks left by other muskies in the glossy paint surface of the wooden lure.

It was enough that fine evening just to be there, and I wasn't fishing seriously; that would keep for the bleak days, when the rain hammered down and the waves lashed against the rocky shores of the lake. I worked the plug along the margin of the weed bed for a while, then shifted my feet slightly and cast over towards a spot where the sheer granite face of the small island indicated a deep pocket.

16

When the Pikie minnow was about half way in to the boat, I felt a slight jolt, then a light tugging transmitted through the rod to my fingers and wrist. I knew what it was — either a small bass or an early-feeding walleye, probably the latter. Nothing to get excited about; almost an annoyance, really. A matter of hoping that the treble hooks had not done too much damage to the audacious little fish, so that it could be released in good shape to live and grow for another day.

I reeled in, almost contemptuously disinterested, allowing plenty of slack in the hope that it would shake free before I had to boat it. Looking down, I could see for some distance out beneath the still surface. The fish came in sight — a pickerel of about a pound or a little more, coming in listlessly, the rear hooks of the lure embedded in its immature jaws. Silly fish, I thought, hitting a plug that big.

I had brought it within ten or twelve feet of the boat when it happened. A shape came charging up out of the weeds — a shape so incredibly huge, so gargantuan, that my jaw dropped and a chill passed over me on that warm evening. I could see the 'lunge clearly; I can still see it clearly, as I write this, all these years later.

The huge, gaping jaws looked like something from pre-historic times. The surface of the water heaved and erupted from the great bulk and the sheer savagery of the attack. I saw the wide-set eyes, the twisting, deep-sided strength of the huge torso, the tinge of orange on the giant tail. That fish was as thick through the back as a tree trunk — and as long as a paddle.

Startled, I involuntarily jerked the rod tip, just enough to snatch the walleye out of reach of the closing jaws.

I started to reel in again, quickly now, feeling a sense of panic, like a boxer who suddenly realizes that he is hopelessly over-matched and that the slugger he is in with knows it. Nobody in the world could have landed that fish alone. I wanted no part of it.

But in the next instant he was back, hurtling up out of the weeds. I stopped reeling, overcome with awe and a sense of helplessness.

There was a frenzied, ferocious churning and threshing near my floating Pikie minnow. Two-thirds of the muskie's great length breached the calm surface of the water, the huge tail lashing violently. And then it was gone, gliding down with incredible speed into the depths.

I reeled in the last few feet of line, lay the rod on the floorboards, and sank weakly down onto the seat. It was a minute or two before I regained enough strength to take my cigarettes out of my shirt pocket. My fingers were shaking as I lit one. I was scared — plain and simply, scared. Shortly I picked up the rod again, and swung the Pikie minnow in so that I could inspect it. The head of the poor little walleye was still on the treble hooks at the back of the plug, but the rest of the fish was gone. The muskie had bitten it off cleanly at the gills, the huge teeth cutting through scales, bones, fins, innards, everything. Usually, underwater predators don't do that — either they swallow a victim whole, or they leave it more or less in shreds because their teeth, however sharp, are irregular and gapped so that they tend to tear at the flesh of their prey. But this monster had had the bite and the power in its jaws to neatly chomp off all it wanted of that pickerel without encountering the hooks of my plug. That seemed somehow supernatural to me, just as the incredible size of the 'lunge was quite unnatural.

I finished the first cigarette, then smoked another. After that, I picked up the oars, fitted them into the locks, and started to row back towards the island. The sun had just gone by then, and it was strange to hear the so-normal sounds of the lake in the slowly fading afterglow — a loon calling out by Roxborough's, a screendoor closing, a dog barking, a gramaphone, a child crying.

Just how big was that 'lunge? Well, I've seen a few muskies in my day, including some lunkers, more than you could count on your fingers and toes, that went upwards of thirty pounds. I mean I wasn't about to start stuttering at the sight of an ordinary trophy fish. But that monster in the narrow channel up at the end of Caseman's Island was at least twice as big, maybe three times as big, as anything I ever saw before or since. If you really want to know the truth, I think that 'lunge would have gone at least a hundred pounds.

As far as I know, it was only ever hooked once — although it probably demolished a lot of tackle without ever showing itself. Just one run, and that would be it, leaving you with the frayed end of a broken casting line.

The following summer my friend Clarence, the guide, was working that inlet with a man and his wife from Akron, Ohio, who were staying at the Crowe's Landing hotel. On about his third cast the man got a strike.

"Never saw the beat of it," Clarence told me on the steps going up to the pavilion that night. His eyes still looked somewhat stunned, and there was an uncharacteristic pallor under his leathery tan.

"Couldn't have been over by the end of Caseman's, could it?"

"Yeah, as a matter of fact, it was. That fish just charged right at us, like he wanted to kill us all. I never been attacked by a fish before, not in all the years."

"So what happened?" I asked

"He went clean over the boat, between me and the couple from Akron. Good people, too. Tipped well."

"The guy lost him, eh?" I asked, already knowing the answer.

"Lost him, hell. Damn 'lunge spit the plug into my lap when he come over the boat."

"You're gonna try for him another time, I bet. Right? Maybe come September."

Clarence snorted. "You crazy?" he asked. "I don't want nothin' to do with a fish as big as me."

4.
Granddad

J.D. — for John Donnelly — was a tall, willowy thin, quiet and basically gentle man who was born in Cavan Township in south-central
Ontario in the year 1870. Nobody in the family knows anything
about his mother and father, but some of us like to think there was
some Indian blood in J.D.'s veins, although that is probably just a
romantic notion on our part. Still, the way he was so at home in the
wilderness, walking through the bush or paddling his canoe, would
make you wonder.

   Granddad was an old man during the years that I remember him.
His hair, white as the crest of a wave in a high wind, was full, and his
long, thin face, though lined and creased, was somehow not an old
face. He was stooped a little, more because of his height and the
generally relaxed way he carried his body, I think, than as a product
of age. His hands and arms were thin and bony, but there was the
strength of a cable in them. Winter and summer, he always wore a
peak cap, usually of some tweed material. He smoked big, heavy,
foul-smelling pipes, and he was the most insatiable reader I ever met;
wherever granddad went, there would be a book close at hand.

   I don't suppose it's usual to remember one's grandfather as a
friend, but that's the way I think of J.D. When I was a boy he used to
take me for a walk every Sunday morning that he was in the city.
Rain or shine, whatever the season. We had a half-dozen favourite
routes — following the abandoned railway right-of-way to Bears'
Creek, along the canal and over the high bridge, beside the river in

the south end of town — and each of them was probably four or five miles long. He would point out things as we strolled along, the old man and the boy, and I learned a lot during those walks. It was a very special kind of Sunday school.

For a great many years J.D. owned a fine furniture store in Peterborough, but he had sold the business by the time I was old enough to tie my own shoelaces. For most of his life, though, and especially after his retirement, J.D.'s real home was at his cottage on an island in Stoney Lake, the easternmost of the Kawartha chain that loops along the Pre-Cambrian Shield in central Ontario. Cottage and store, lake and city, might only be twenty-five miles apart, but for Grandad the real distance couldn't be ascertained by studying the map; the one he endured through economic necessity, the other he loved.

Simply stated, J.D. lived for that lake. The five months of each year, from mid-November to mid-April, during which snow and ice and sub-zero, tree-cracking cold made it impossible to survive on the island, constituted an annual period of purgatory which must, somehow, be endured. His wife, my grandmother, had died a couple of years before he decided to give up the store. After that, he would wait impatiently each late winter while the local hockey playoffs wound down, and the high-piled snows trickled away, and patches of grass bared and grew greener, and the birds began to come back. And then, one morning he would be gone, hitching rides for his more than three score year-old body, or paying some local to drive him to the shore of his beloved lake. Grandad never did have a car of his own, although I suppose he could have afforded one, for the same reason that he never bought an outboard motor; mechanical contrivances were just not his style.

Deposited on the shore of the lake — his lake — he would wait there, at peace then in the warming spring sunshine, his canoe pulled up beside him on the bank — a few hours, a day, a week, perhaps even two — until the ice went out. That might be with a roar, the big cakes crushing docks and boathouses as if they were made of cardboard. Or, more often, the sodden, leaden seal of winter would simply sink, belatedly, with an anti-climactic sigh.

Whatever the particulars of winter's ultimate denouement, Granddad's canoe would be on the lake almost before the open season's first ripple or wave, and he would cook his supper in the kitchen of the cottage that evening. There he would remain through the lengthening days of April, May, and June, seeing the annual return of the loons, watching the spring flowers break through the sere, brown leaves, luxuriating in the maturing, new growth around the margin of the lake. Later on, his sons and their wives and children and the rest of the summer colony would arrive, to bask in the benevolent bounty of July and August. And then, golden September, next to June the best time of all, and alone again. October, and the reds and yellows and golds melting into russet browns. Geese honking overhead against the fiery, purple-streaked twilight sky. A morning, finally, when the loons were gone. The bare greyness of November. Frost on the pine needles on the path down to the boathouse. Ice skimming the surface of the little harbour at the back, where he dipped for his pails of water.

And at last, reluctantly, heavy-heartedly, nailing on the shutters, locking the door of the cottage, and going back to the always alien city in an attempt to outlast the long, restricting months of winter one more time.

Around Christmas each year J.D. would look plain old, rather than just elderly, and you would see the frailty in the thin, slightly stooped shoulders, and notice that he seemed withdrawn, his mind appearing to wander now and then; and you would think, feeling somehow a little guilty for having the thought, that winter was about to win at last, and that granddad had probably stepped on his beloved island for the final time.

And then, as the days gradually lengthened, and the gutters ran in the warming spring sunshine, and people began to keep an eye open for the first robin, miraculous physiological and mental changes would start to take place in Granddad. Sometimes the miracle would unfold slowly, sometimes it would take place between breakfast and dinner in a single day. The infirm shuffle of January and February, which made you worry about a fall and the possibility of a broken hip, would once again become a firm stride. J.D., instead of sleeping until noon, would be up early each morning, proclaiming the virtues of a good breakfast, and head off downtown on mysterious missions before the sun had risen high enough to renew its attack on the dwindling snow that remained on the western slopes of the buildings which lined the main street. Young as we were, my two cousins and I, we would become aware of a mounting impatience in the elderly man. And in his room he would day-by-day accumulate the things he would need to reopen the cottage for another post-purgatory season — new batteries for his flashlight, wicks for the coaloil lamps, cans of paint, a store of pipe tobacco, wooden matches, books to be read, dried beans to be baked. And one morning about the middle of April he would be gone again . . . .

Sometimes townspeople — busybodies, mostly — would ask my father and his brother if they "really thought it was right" to leave granddad up there alone on that isolated island at his age; weren't we afraid that "something might happen to him?" And my dad would just smile, and say that, of course, something *was* going to happen to him, sooner or later, and where better for it to happen than at the lake? Sure, he could be looked after, and kept well fed and warm in the city; but does a bull moose, antlers grown heavy with his years, deserve to wind up in a zoo?

Early in November one autumn J.D. went out behind the cottage to chop some kindling for the next morning's fire. It was a raw, windy night, and he propped the flashlight in the cross-tree of the saw-horse so that he could see what he was doing. The flashlight slipped just as the hatchet-head was descending, and in the sudden darkness the sharp blade all but severed the tip of the index finger on his left hand.

J.D. went back inside the cottage. The pain must have been excruciating, and there would have been a lot of blood. The finger tip was hanging by a few shreds of skin. He took stock of the situation. The nearest neighbor was two miles across the lake at Crowe's Landing. Or he could paddle to the near shore and walk the three miles out to the highway. He knew that he would almost certainly pass out before he could complete either trip.

So he put the finger tip back in place, and fastened it as best he could with strips of adhesive tape. Then he rigged a tourniquet with a dish cloth and a wooden mixing spoon, took a few aspirins, poured a stiff drink, and resigned himself to sitting up through the long night; to fall asleep was almost certainly to bleed to death.

In the morning, the situation appearing to have stabilized somewhat, he paddled the hundred yards to the shore and started to walk out to the highway. A mile or so further on, a local farmer picked him up and drove him to Lakefield, some twenty miles away. The doctor there sewed the finger tip back on, doing so only at granddad's insistence and against the doctor's better judgement. The doctor's professional opinion was that the finger could not be reunited, not after the passage of so many hours, not on a man of granddad's age. The doctor was wrong; J.D. was using that fingertip to tamp tobacco into the bowl of his pipe by mid-January of the following winter.

To employ a term that he would never have understood, granddad had his own, distinctive life style. He read constantly, more than anybody I ever knew, except perhaps for my father. In the summer months he always kept a pair of binoculars handy — ostensibly in order to study the wonders of nature, but really in case a pretty girl happened to appear on the horizon. In spite of his thin frame, he had an appetite like a lumberjack, with a particular affection for blueberry pie. He smoked pipes so scarred, pitted and malodorous that they might have been in constant use since the days of Sir Walter Raleigh. He was not what could be called a drinking man, but every afternoon about five o'clock he poured himself a glass of scotch — not a shot but a full tumbler.

One summer there was a terrible heatwave, the thermometer climbing to over one hundred degrees for five or six days in a row. One of those nights I was lying in bed, the sheet under me damp with perspiration, trying to will myself to sleep. A brilliant moon was shining from a cloudless sky. Not a breath of air stirred the curtains beside the screened windows. And on the mainland, a hundred yards or so across the dead calm water from the island, a bull frog was serenading the night, his deep-throated, constant 'Ma-room, ma-room, ma-room' sounding absurdly loud, like the hyper-amplified cacaphony of a rock group, and ensuring that no one within hearing of his chorus would find succor in the arms of Morpheus on that mercilessly hot and humid night. From the occasional creaking of the bed springs in his room, a couple of doors removed from mine, I knew that granddad, too, was enduring a restless, sleepless time.

It must have been about two o'clock in the morning when I heard J.D. get up. Lying there, with the moonlight washing the beaver-board walls of my room, what happened next came to me like radio as opposed to TV — I could hear, but not see, what was going on.

The sound of granddad's door closing. Footsteps. The keel of the canoe grating slightly as it was pushed off the sand of the little beach. Then the small sounds an accomplished canoeist makes — the dip . . . dip and drip . . . drip . . . drip of the paddle, gradually receding.

The overpowering, monotonous, the-hell-with-you chorus of the bull frog, filling the still night. The receding, small sounds of the canoe.

Then a single, shattering blast, echoing off the mainland hill behind the cottage. Granddad's ancient, single-barrel 16-gauge shotgun.

Then complete, merciful silence. No more 'Ma-room, ma-room, ma-room.'

Finally, the canoe returning, granddad's bedroom door opening and closing, a last creaking of bedsprings. Peace.

Once or twice each summer J.D. would take me out bass fishing in the white skiff. Learning to fish from him was like taking a course in creative writing given by William Shakespeare. He had a ten-foot long, split bamboo rod, a thing of delicate strength and superb craftsmanship, which most of the time reposed on the rafters of the boathouse. I don't know where he got it, or how long he had had it, but I'm sure that it was much older, even, than he. To guess, it probably dated from the third-quarter of the nineteenth century. The handle was fitted with a simple, hand-made, narrow-spool reel of approximately equal antiquity.

When we were anchored alongside one of his favourite bass holes, granddad would manipulate that apparently unwieldy and cumbersome rig with the sureness and lightness of touch of a true artist. It was he who first revealed to me the irresistibility of a properly presented grasshopper to a hungry smallmouth bass. But, whatever live bait we were using — crayfish, dew worms, white grubs, minnows, grasshoppers — he would delicately work the slender tip of that ancient rod, never using more than three or four feet of free line, and drop the tasty offering into a pocket in the weeds, or alongside a rock shelf or sunken log, practically under the nose of a waiting smallmouth. Nowadays, most bass fishermen you see sit huddled over their stubby casting or spinning rods, dangling their lifeless bait straight down into ten or twelve feet of water. Granddad would have shaken his head in wonderment at that; he knew that you have to keep working the bait, and that you've got to get it into the shallows. To him it was simple: where would a hungry bass go to search for food — to the dark and lifeless bottom of the lake, or around the bountiful in-shore waters? Hell, when you want to eat, you don't crawl under the cottage; you go to the kitchen, where the food is.

But, although a superb bass fisherman, willing to indulge his

Grandson a couple of times each summer, J.D. secretly considered the muskie to be the only quarry worth pursuing on a regular basis. I think he was happiest and most complete when he was out alone in his canoe, trolling along some part of the mainland shore or out among the islands. His method was probably adopted from the Indians, and, in the last quarter of the twentieth century, nobody is ever likely to see it employed again. No rod was used, just a sturdy, cotton hand-line, perhaps an eight of an inch thick and strong enough to use for hanging out the Monday wash. At the business end would be a huge double spoon, the blades about the size and shape of poplar leaves, and a large treble hook, partially disguised by partridge feathers or a clump of deer hair. Instead of a reel he relied upon a wooden holder which he had fashioned himself from a piece of one-inch board, about a foot long by four inches wide, whittled to be somewhat narrower at the middle, rounded off at the edges, and with fairly shallow V's fashioned out of both ends. The line was tied securely aroung the waist of the board, then wound lengthwise, the points of the V's keeping it from slipping off.

When trolling alone with both hands busy on the paddle, J.D. would hold the heavy cotton line in his teeth. When a fish struck, he would set down the paddle and haul the muskie in hand-over-hand, the accumulating line coiling on the floorboards in front of him.

The method was not without its perils. Once a big 'lunge struck with such force that J.D.'s uppers were wrenched clean out of his mouth. Fortunately, they bounced off the gunwale and skidded up into the bow of the canoe, where they came to rest, undamaged. Under-standably, that particular fish got away, but Granddad could be counted on to bring in eight or ten good muskies a summer. Anything under about twelve pounds, he threw back — "to give it a chance to grow up."

Aside from storing the line when not in use, the wooden 'reel' served an additional purpose. If the spoon got caught on a shoal, J.D. would just spit out the line, and reach down and toss the piece of wood overboard. Then he could turn around at his leisure, go back and retrieve the floating 'buoy', and have plenty of slack line with which to free his snagged lure.

That block, as Granddad used to call it, figured prominently in one of the wildest muskie escapades I remember from all those long-ago summers. About noon one August day, Granddad and I and my cousin Alex set out in the white skiff to make the two mile trip through the islands to Crowe's Landing, on the south shore of the lake. It was a very windy day, with the threat of a storm in the air, and we wouldn't have gone except that it was 'butcher day,' and we were out of meat. Every summer Tuesday a panel truck, operated by a butcher from the nearest town, parked for a couple of hours on the dock at the landing, its van loaded with chops, steaks, roasts, bacon, sausages, stewing beef and whole bolognas, kept fresh by hundred pound blocks of ice. To miss that weekly visit was to subsist on a diet of beans, salt pork and fish for the next seven days.

So we left the island, Alex and I rowing, Gramps in the stern, with a paddle in the crook of his right arm, to take care of the steering. Alex and I were both about thirteen or fourteen at the time. Rowing in tandem, you could usually make that skiff walk across the water, but it was hard work that day, with those big swells rolling up out of the west. Naturally, near-gale or no near-gale, J.D. had the hand troll out ; no reason to miss a chance at a 'lunge.

We were almost through the islands, better than halfway across, with one final point to clear before we started the last stretch across open water to the Landing. There are some shoals off that promontory, and we had to beat up into the wind before we could swing wide around them. It was really blowing by then, the odd whitecap breaking over the bow, and Alex and I were putting all the strength of our youthful backs into it. Then, just as we came abreast of the rocks, something almost tore the line from Granddad's hand.

"We're snagged !" J.D. shouted, tossing the wooden block over the side. "Bring her around ! Look smart now !"

Alex and I each backed on one oar and pulled with the other, pivoting the bow and stern until we were heading back downwind.

"Where's that block ?" Granddad yelled. "Do you see it boys ?"

We peered around at the angry sea.

"There she goes, Gramps !" Alex shouted suddenly.

"Where ? Where ?"

"Heading for Northey's Bay," Alex told him.

It was, too, skipping across the waves like a miniature PT boat, going like a bat out of the boathouse eaves.

"After it ! After it !" Granddad was already digging the blade of his paddle in, to help swing the bow back up into the wind.

For a while it seemed that the muskie was going to tear right through the Boschink Channel, hell-bent for Juniper Island. Pulling at the oars until our arms ached, Alex and I had to fight for every yard against the mounting gale.

"Faster! Faster!" J.D. implored us.

After what was probably five minutes, but seemed much longer, the fish finally stopped to rest.

"Now we'll get him," Granddad said, leaning forward eagerly in his stern seat.

But, just as we were pulling up alongside the block, it took off again, this time in the opposite direction.

"Come about! Come about!" Granddad instructed us.

Then we were off again, the big rollers now sweeping us along like a surf board off the coast of Oahu. Once more we almost caught up with it, only to have it veer off on a new tack. Again and again the sequence was repeated. Back and forth we went, all over that end of the lake. Anyone watching from shore would have concluded that we had gone mad, and it would have been difficult to argue the point. After a while Alex and I were just rowing from memory, reacting automatically to the shouted commands from astern. The clouds had closed down on the lake by then, and a driving, cold rain lashed over us. But J.D. was not about to give up, not with a good fish on the end of the line.

Finally, on what must have been the ninth or tenth pass, we got close enough for Granddad to pick the block off the crest of a wave. You'd think that 'lunge would have been worn out by then — God knows, Alex and I were — but he still had plenty of fight left in him, and it was another few minutes before J.D. was able to swing him in over the gunwale.

When we weighed him on the scales at Crowe's Landing, he went just a shade over 22 pounds — not a record by any means but, as Gramps said, "a pretty good average." By that time the butcher had departed the wharf for another week, but J.D.'s friend, old Bob, sold us some steaks from the ice box in the hotel kitchen, at cost. As a fellow fisherman, he understood that first things have to be put first.

There were still quite a few 'lunge to come after that for J.D. He caught the last one, fishing alone, of course, in his canoe, late in August of the summer before he died. He was then eighty-two — or maybe eighty-four or eighty-seven, depending on how he felt at the time he might condescend to talk about it.

28

As far as I can remember, he was never sick a day in his life. Then, one cold February night, he died in his sleep at my uncle's house. I'm sure he had had his customary glass of scotch late that final afternoon.

When he was tidying up the few effects Granddad kept in the city, my uncle found a list J.D. had begun to compile of the things he would need to take with him to the lake, come that spring that never came.

Like my dad used to say, every man should be lucky enough to have an island, either a real one or one in his dreams.

5.

Speckled Trout for the Blue Watch

During World War II, I put in four quite ordinary and non-heroic years in the RCNVR (Royal Canadian Naval Voluntary Reserve) as one of the tens of thousands of young men of draft age who enlisted in the navy primarily to evade the still less attractive prospect of being conscripted into the army. During basic training the powers-that-were decided, in their elusive wisdom, that I should be a wireless operator — a decision probably arrived at through a process of elimination since, while it was quite clear that I couldn't do much of anything else to enhance the naval war effort, there was no irrefutable evidence at hand that I might not eventually be able to cope with the Morse code.

After that, like everyone else in uniform, I spent most of the time standing in line-ups — waiting to eat, waiting to have teeth filled, waiting to be immunized from God knows what diseases, waiting to have my papers stamped, waiting for re-assignment to other line-ups. There was a lot of marching, although no one ever explained why sailors had to learn to march, unless it was to be able to walk on water, should the need ever arise. There was some canteen duty, and some leave. There was the business of learning how to communicate with dots and dashes — for which, to establish that recruiting officers were not *always* wrong, I turned out to have considerable aptitude.

There were, eventually, some months on the North Atlantic — first in a prematurely-aged corvette, later in a spanking new frigate.

Wallowing convoys. Endless, indistinguishable days. The bleak, inhospitable sea. Depth charges. A periscope in the chill mists of dawn. Liberty ships, going down by the stern. Tankers, spilling their burning intestines across the leaden swells. Londonderry, Ireland. Reykjavik, Iceland, a couple of times. Through the gate in the anti-submarine nets beneath Telegraph Hill, and into the rugged sanctuary of the harbour of St. John's, Newfoundland. Fog, and rain, and cold, and dreariness, and monotony.

And then, for eighteen months, from the late fall of 1943 to the late spring of 1945, there was the very best time.

Early in the war the Canadian Navy had built a ship-shore wireless station in Newfoundland, near a crossroads called Bay Bulls, eight or ten miles east of St. John's. It was one of a network of twenty-five or thirty such stations which girdled the globe and incorporated such romantic-sounding and far away places as Gibraltar, Sydney, Aden and Karachi. Collectively these stations handled all the radio traffic with the Allied ships at sea, maintaining a constant, twenty-four hour-a-day watch on a half-dozen or so frequencies. It was important work because many of the messages — "signals," they were called in the navy — involved high priority and emergency matters such as distress calls and enemy sighting reports. And it required considerable skill, both in mastering the intricacies of the global communications system and in getting the ships off the air as quickly as possible to minimize the danger of their transmissions being zeroed in on by enemy direction-finding equipment. A lot of the time others may have wondered whether what they were doing was either necessary or useful, but at the Bay Bulls' wireless station we had no such doubts, and it was a good feeling to know that your contribution really mattered.

Both the physical amenities and the prevailing atmosphere were almost idyllic for the navy in wartime. Because the complement was small (under fifty) and semi-permanent, you got to know your shipmates very well; nobody locked their lockers, and if someone was going off watch, and needed five bucks, he would take it — and you would know that you would get it back come payday. We had a well-equipped recreation room, a good canteen, outdoor volleyball and basketball courts, and first-run movies every Friday night. The cook and his helper ignored the official menus distributed by Naval Headquarters, and did their best to give us what we liked to eat; you could always go into the galley and raid the refrigerator, or heat up any delicacies you had received in packages from home.

There was a delightful absence of the mindless, by-the-book discipline that you ran into at most shore bases. The boss, a Lieutenant-Commander, was a decent, sensible man who had an apartment in St. John's, and was only on hand for five or six hours a day, Mondays through Fridays. The rest of the time the place was run by three of the best Petty Officers, two Canadians and one Londoner, ever to draw a tot of rum. The result was that we could wear what we liked, do what we liked, say what we liked — so long as we did our jobs well. The one thing they would not tolerate was carelessness while on duty; like the rest of us, they had a lot of friends at sea, and they knew that what we did in the signals room on the second floor could mean the difference between life and death out there on the convoy routes. Thus the emphasis was where it should be, on what mattered, and we respected that intelligence and responded to it.

We did put in long hours. As in every other naval establishment, at sea or on land, the ship's company at the wireless station was divided into three watches — red, white and blue. We worked on the basis of two days on duty, and one day off. Each tour began at noon on one day, and concluded at 8 a.m. the second morning following. During those two days (apart from the two-hour dog watches) it was alternately four hours on, and four off, so that you had to learn to sleep quickly and in short snatches. It seemed that you were forever getting up. The third day, actually twenty-eight hours — from 8 a.m. one day until twelve noon the next — was yours to do with as you saw fit. Sometimes we would go into St. John's in search of whatever diversions we could find. Other times we would stay at the station on our days off — to tend to domestic chores like washing and mending, to write overdue letters home, to play some volleyball or basketball or horseshoes, or merely to catch up on sleep.

It was during one of those respites for the blue watch — mine — that I discovered the little lake, nestled among the bald, Newfoundland hills, across from the station. You had to cross some fields, and then find your way through thick cedar thickets to get to it, and from the road, a half-mile away, you would never have known that it was there.

The lake was of miniature proportions — no more than a quarter of a mile long, and less than fifty yards across at its widest point. It appeared to be spring-fed, the water crystal clear and very cold. So peaceful and undisturbed was that lake, so alone there at the base of the coastal hills, that it was easy, though of course inaccurate, to feel that you might be the first human being ever to look across it.

When you think about the island province, 'beautiful' is probably not one of the adjectives that come immediately to mind. Certainly the district in which the Navy had elected to plump down its wireless station had few of the characteristics of a paradise. The trees were spindly and stunted. The landscape, in the lea of the hills, was mostly flat and generally bleak. The soil was shallow, sandy, rocky and parsimonious, and God knows how the few families who lived along the road eked out a living. Their houses were small, frail and dispirited-looking, the clapboard always in dire need of paint. Some of the children from those homes used to come to the station to watch the movies we ran every Friday evening. They would just appear out of the fog that seemed to hang over the land for so much of the time, sit through the picture, never talking or laughing or showing any reactions whatever, and then they would leave as silently as they had arrived. They were never impolite and they were always welcome, but there was a kind of sad emptiness in their innocent faces, as if they were already old before they had had a chance to be young. Their parents were warm-hearted and generous with what little they had to give, and tapped mysterious, seemingly bottomless reservoirs of humour so that they were almost always cheerful. Maybe their strength of spirit filtered into them from the sea; it certainly couldn't have derived from the sterile, inhospitable land that was theirs.

And yet that little lake, when I came upon it that first time, on an early evening in mid-June, with the sun dappling its deep blue, breeze-ruffled surface, was one of the purest, most totally unspoiled, most idealistically beautiful places my eyes have ever encountered. A few gulls shrieked and scolded at the far end, but otherwise there was no sound to infringe upon the silence. The shore was natural pastureland on my side, but across the lake the cedars crowded down to the edge, oddly tailored in shape, like trimmed, ornamental plantings around a pond in a sophisticated urban park.

I had come to realize by then that Newfoundland had some great trout fishing to offer. A couple of us had stood on a bridge over the creek in Bowering Park, on the outskirts of St. John's, one Sunday afternoon, and watched fish of four and five pounds hovering in the shadows — while sailors strolled by with their girlfriends, and families had picnics all around. And I had heard stories of how you could catch speckles big enough for the pan in even the most insignificant of the streams that cut across the island's few roads.

And so, when I stumbled upon it, it was only natural that I should wonder if there were any trout in the little jewel of a lake across from the wireless station. I did not, of course, have any equipment with me, but I was overcome with curiosity — and excitement — and I had to find out. But what to use for bait? It was early June, and it would be two months before there were any grasshoppers around. I turned over some stones, looking for whatever I could find, but to no avail. Then, further up on the bank, I came upon an old, rotted tree stump. Kicking away at it with the heel of my shoe, I uncovered a nest of fat white grubs — probably June bug larvae. I put a half-dozen of them into my flat, round navy cap, and went back down to the water's edge.

I threw the first one about twenty feet out into the lake. Almost before the ripples had started to form on the surface of the water, a trout came up out of the cold, clear depths and took it. I thought it might go eleven or twelve inches, and maybe a little over a half-pound. It had had to move quickly to beat four or five of its friends or relatives to the offering. The rest of the white grubs were also snatched up, as fast as I could throw them into the water.

A week or so later I talked about the lake to Gus, the nearby resident who drove the one-ton truck which served double-duty as the wireless station's supply vehicle and bus. He allowed as how there were "some trouts in that lake, not too big, mind you," and offered to lend me some tackle. What he subsequently provided was an ancient, nine or ten foot, split bamboo rod, not unlike the one my grandfather used for bass, forty or fifty feet of silk casting line, a few split-shot, and a couple of light, long-shanked hooks, about number nine or ten. It was hardly a classic trout fishing outfit but, as Gus no doubt realized, and as subsequent developments were to prove, it was quite adequate for the virgin trout in the little lake at the foot of the Bay Bulls' hills.

Gus had become a good friend of mine by then, and I tried several times to talk him into going fishing with me, but he always declined.

"No, buy," he'd say, "trouts is for when you've got nothin' else to do, and Gus is too busy now for any of that."

The backwater of the war had given him a job such as he had

never had before, with regular paychecks, and for the first time a chance to plan ahead, and he felt that any dalliance, however innocent, might somehow imperil the unexpected windfall. And so he stuck to his menial job, performing it most conscientiously, and with great dignity. Meanwhile, the little lake would be there for Gus, as it has always been, for some future time.

I went there often during the rest of the summer and the early fall of the year 1944. Sometimes the sun shone, as it had done that first day; more often the clouds hung low over the barren, rugged hills, and the mists swirled down to the surface of the lake. Always there was the feeling of peace, and indescribable loneliness, and personal discovery. Always there was the magic. And always I took trout — no trophy fish, but a seemingly inexhaustible supply of silvery, speckled, blunt-headed beauties which ran under a pound and made magnificent eating when fried in butter — which, in spite of the rationing back home, was always in plentiful supply for us.

I used small, red worms, dug from behind the wireless station, during the early part of the season, but switched to grasshoppers — the world's best bait for trout and bass — as soon as they became available, towards the end of July. The big, flying variety — black or grey outside, bright yellow under their wings — were the most effective, and I'd catch them in the cool of evening, when they are lethargic, and put them in a milk bottle with a perforated top. (You have about as much chance of catching them in the heat of the day, when they spook easily and fly all over the landscape, as you would have of catching trout by swimming after them.) When you tossed one of those big 'hoppers out on the surface of the lake, with its wings fluttering to show flashes of yellow, you could count on getting a strike nine times out of ten. I never used a sinker, letting the weight of the line take the bait down slowly, and it seldom sank very far before something took it.

About the middle of August I offered to provide fresh trout for breakfast some morning for our whole blue watch, all eight operators and the London P.O., Newell, who was in charge of us. The idea was accepted with enthusiasm, and it was agreed that we would do it when we came off watch at eight o'clock at the end of our next two-day tour of duty. There was one frequency, 12685 kilocycles, on which reception was extremely marginal during the hours around dawn so that there was very little traffic during the last two hours of the morning watch. If we turned up the volume on that set, the P.O. could monitor it, which would leave one operator — me — free to do more productive things.

In a way that was typical of the staff at the wireless station, the idea caught on, and quickly developed into a festive event. The cook agreed to prepare the feast, and offered to provide plenty of home fried potatoes and a couple of pounds of sausages for the occasion. Someone else donated a magnificent canned ham he had received in a package from home — ideal for slicing and frying. Another watch-mate contributed three dozen fresh eggs, obtained from a local farmer by bartering a quart of high-proof, navy rum. And so on.

The morning of that day dawned fresh and clear, the sun coming up into a cloudless sky, and with just enough nip in the air to remind you that fall was only a few weeks away in that northern latitude. I reached the shore of the lake a little after six, when the sun was just easing up over the treetops. There was a slight mist rising from the surface of the water, which the sun would soon burn off.

Something unexpected had happened to underscore the occasion with pathos. An hour earlier we had received a signal informing us that one of the veteran Canadian corvettes, a battle-scarred old pro, had been torpedoed and sunk with no survivors. Her name had been so long familiar that we all took it as a personal loss, a death in the family. Most of us had known at least one of the ship's company that had gone down with her.

You had to shrug it off, of course, and go on, except perhaps to drink a toast to her some maudlin midnight. It was not the first time something like that had happened, nor would it be the last. There was particular difficulty that morning in making the two things fit in my mind as parts of the same scheme of things — the serene, innocent, almost virginal beauty of the little lake, sparkling in the early morning sunshine, and the knowledge that, just over those mist-shrouded hills, wreckage drifted and friends had died in the alien, grey wastes of the North Atlantic.

Fortunately, to take my mind off the larger world, the trout were hitting with even more gusto than usual. The bait would land lightly on the surface, then begin to sink slowly into the cold, clear, azure-blue depths. A shape, torpedo-like in its speed, yet somehow fluid and graceful rather than hard and deadly, would come charging up to take it. Then a few graceful, athletic runs, the trout darting and dancing across the sun-flecked surface, the rod-tip bending in answer, and soon another unbelievably clean, colour-splashed beauty would join the growing string on the dew-bejewelled grass behind me.

Less than an hour later I was back at the station with a couple of dozen ten to fourteen-inch trout. The cook and I cleaned them, and a little after eight, when the blue watch was relieved and came down from the second-floor signals room, breakfast was ready.

It was a feast fit for emperors and sultans. Perhaps spurred on by the need to forget the other business, the cook and I had scurried around to add the finishing touches which transformed a memorable breakfast into a bacchanalian orgy. He had broken open the officers' Stores to provide white linen tablecloths, real silverware, even candles. I had liberated a secret cache of navy-issue rum in order to appropriately spike our morning coffee.

When my watch-mates came into the mess deck, the scene that greeted them was straight out of a Hollywood movie about Henry VIII. Stacks of hot, buttered toast. Mounds of creamy scrambled eggs. Crisp bacon by the pound, browned sausages, piles of slightly curled, sugar-cured ham. Fried, sliced, green tomatoes. Bowls of charred, home fried potatoes. Pitchers full of fresh orange juice. Jugs of rum. Gallons of hot coffee. And, the piece-de-resistance: two dozen, pinkish-golden, freshly caught speckled trout.

As it happened, one member of the blue watch had a guest that morning, a seaman in the U.S. Navy, whose destroyer was in drydock at the American base at Argentia, permitting him to spend the night at the wireless station. I'll never forget the look on his face when he came in to breakfast, his mouth wide-open when he saw what was laid out before him. He was particularly impressed by the apparently limitless supply of rum, and the fresh-from-the-water speckled trout. He said that the only fish *his* navy ever supplied was precariously frozen, often wormy, halibut.

Mutually aware that it is bad manners to disillusion a guest, we conspired together in the fiction that it was just the routine start to an ordinary, normal day. Nobody said or did anything to suggest that there was anything special about the bountiful gourmet spread.

And to this day, when he can find someone to listen to his war memoirs — a polite grandchild, perhaps, or an amiable drunk in a bar — he no doubt still talks about the time he stayed at a Canadian Navy wireless station in Newfoundland.

"Ate like kings," he might say. "Damned if I know how a country like Canada could afford it. Imagine — fresh trout for breakfast every morning!!"

6.
Fresh Fish:
A Thousand Dollars a Pound

In a way, this story will be cheating, because it has almost nothing to do with the gentle art, hallowed sport, profound science, or whatever other noble claims you might want to make for the angling pursuit, as it has been traditionally practiced by 'gentlemen.' It will, as a matter of fact, take you about as far away as you might be willing to go from such esoteric pretensions, and owes nothing to the genteel and very special sense of fulfilment which presumably comes from expertly working a hand-tied dry fly across the surface of an expensively-leased pool on some New Brunswick salmon river.

On the other hand, *most* Canadians are genetically conditioned by the broad but grudging, stingy land they occupy to fish for meat, to go down to the rivers and lakes in order to 'put something on the table.' And, in this latter sense, the story of HMCS *Chemong's* fish feed is about as generic to this country as the fact that, until very recently, boys and girls of elementary school age had to file in by separate entrances in order to reach their classrooms.

During World War II, Canada's soldiers, sailors and airmen rarely had fresh fish to eat, regardless of the theatres in which they might be called upon to serve. The brook trout which wound up gracing the breakfast table at our wireless station in Newfoundland were about as typical as extra dry martinis before supper at the Mission of the Little Sisters of the Poor.

39

In St. John's, Newfoundland, during the war you could buy halibut or cod, caught that morning, for about twenty-five cents per whole fish at dockside. Naturally, the braintrust responsible for navy provisioning declined to buy them. Instead, the fish served at Canadian naval establishments in Newfoundland every Friday came via Montreal. Oh, it was certainly caught in Newfoundland waters. But then, for reasons beyond the comprehension of ordinary men, it was transported to the Quebec metropolis, where it was cleaned, filleted, packed in wooden cases in ice, and shipped back to St. John's, arriving there anywhere from six weeks to six months after it was hauled from the sea — and at a per pound cost approximately equal to that of Beluga caviar. By then it was as tasteless as blotting paper, as soggy as a swamp, and as popular in mess decks as liver and bacon.

There was this one time, however, when the cook on the HMCS *Chemong* beat the system. The *Chemong* was a well-travelled, veteran Canadian minesweeper, attached at that time to a mid-Atlantic escort group, operating between St. John's, Newfoundland, and Londonderry, Northern Ireland. In addition to the *Chemong*, the group consisted of four corvettes and a somewhat battle-scarred frigate, which was the senior ship. All six escort vessels belonged to the wartime Canadian navy.

On one westbound trip the *Chemong* and its fellow naval ships turned a convoy of merchantmen and tankers over to a local escort group, which would shepherd it into Halifax, Boston and New York, and broke off to make port in St. John's, Newfoundland, a hundred miles or so to the north. About half-way there the asdic on the frigate picked up an echo which suggested the presence of a German U-boat, a sounding which was confirmed by one of the corvettes.

The Senior Officer of the escort group on the frigate almost literally rubbed his hands in anticipation. A U-boat, apparently stationary and on the ocean floor in an attempt to escape detection — and no lumbering, frustrating convoy to worry about! An unfettered, once-in-a-lifetime, pure attack situation! The rare kind of an opportunity upon which naval careers are founded!

Now, it must be reported that this particular Senior Officer was not exactly an obvious candidate for a Rhodes scholarship or a Nobel prize. In fact, among the veteran, rank-and-file members of his escort group, he was regarded with something far short of veneration, and disrespectfully, albeit descriptively, referred to as 'One-cell.'

Nevertheless, recognizing a unique chance for advancement when he saw one, and being a keen student of standard naval tactics, he responded quite impressively to the situation. It chanced to be a benevolent, moonlit night, with the sea atypically calm. A buoy was dropped over the location of the presumed U-boat. The ships of the escort group formed up behind the frigate. One by one, on signal from the senior ship, they bore down on the buoy, engines at flank speed, bow waves curling high, pennants flying. Then, at the critical moment, depth charges tumbled off the stern, others arcing out from the throwers on the quarterdeck. It was a scene right out of one of those patriotic movies, designed to help the sale of war bonds, which can still occasionally be seen on the late show, a scene calling for the United States Naval Academy band and chorus to render *Anchors Aweigh* in the background.

The bombardment went on all night, the ratings on the *Chemong* and the other escort ships being at action stations for something like fourteen straight hours. Hundreds of depth-charges were dropped, each pattern sending thousands of tons of water erupting into the bright moonlight. God knows how much was added to the national debt that night. What was for sure was that we certainly blasted the hell out of whatever was down there on the ocean floor. You would think that those in charge of our grand strategy might have wondered why the U-boat didn't try to make a run for it, with all those tons of high explosive dropping around it, but apparently the thought didn't occur to them. Or maybe they were simply having too much fun.

When dawn finally came and we had exhausted our supply of depth charges the sea was literally carpeted with assorted flotsam and countless thousands of dead or stunned fish. Anyone with a reasonable sense of balance could have walked on the water, probably clear through the gates into St. John's harbour.

After a break for breakfast, the Senior Officer of the escort group left his frigate in the Captain's boat to inspect the debris, looking for proof of the U-boat kill. All eyes were on the small craft as it nosed through the floating residue from the long night's dramatic activity. Now and again the boat would stop briefly while some promising bit of evidence was fished out of the sea.

The search went on for a long time, an hour or more. Then, quite abruptly, it ended. The Captain's boat broke off its survey of the wreckage, swung sharply about, and headed back towards the host frigate at full speed. A few minutes later the escort ships were under way, resuming their heading for St. John's harbour, which haven they reached without further incident early that afternoon.

It was a few days later before the full story circulated through the mess decks of the ships tied up alongside the naval jetties in St. John's. Pursuing his exploration the morning after the attack, the Senior Officer of the escort group had finally turned up a portion of a wooden doorframe. There is not, of course, very much that it is wooden in a highly functional, wartime submarine. This particular oaken fragment had incorporated a lock mechanism which, once the rust had been cleared away, could be seen to bear the stamped legend: 'Made in Sheffield, England.' What the escort ships had been blasting to smithereens throughout that long night turned out to have been a British merchantman, clearly long sunk, and most likely gone to her grave through natural causes.

Hitler probably never learned of that particular fiasco, which is probably just as well. Had he done so he might logically have come to the conclusion that the Third Reich couldn't lose the war at sea, and thus been encouraged to hold out longer than he did. On the other hand, though, he might have laughed himself to death there and then, instead of living to swallow a cyanide capsule in the Berlin bunker at a considerably later date.

The affair did, however, have one happy outcome. The Chief Cook on the *Chemong* was a man who took real pride in providing his charges with the best food available. He was also a guy who could recognize an opportunity when one presented itself.

Thus, while the Senior Officer was pursuing his abortive treasure hunt through the wreckage, Cooky retrieved as many floating cod and halibut as came within reach of his eager pike-pole. Subsequently filleted, egg-and-bread-crummed, and fried in plenty of butter, they provided a memorable fish-feed for the crew of the *Chemong* that day, as the minesweeper steamed towards St. John's with the other ships of the escort group.

Canadian taxpayers would have been glad to know that at least something was salvaged for the box-car full of their money that went down the drain that night.

7.
Auntie Belle's First Fish

It was on the Saturday evening of a Labour Day weekend not long after World War II and we were just finishing dinner at the cottage my wife's family had at a remote, northwestern Ontario lake. The lake, just across the Ontario-Manitoba border, was called Malachi, so the story goes, because it was the last section-point in Ontario as the CNR mainline stretched west. It was — and still is — frequented almost exclusively by Winnipeg people. You could only get in by train, and the fishing — for Northern pike, walleyes and bass — was spectacular. A friend of mine and I once took a dozen casts each one June, when the pickerel are always particularly co-operative in that part of the country, and boated twenty fish. There are Northerns in there as big as barracuda, and just about as mean. I know a couple of spots in that lake where anything less than a three-and-a-half pound smallmouth is considered precocious and an annoying interruption to the really serious fishing.

Auntie Belle, who was probably in her early sixties then, and remains one of my all-time favourite people, was spending one of her all too infrequent weekends at the cottage. Kind, gentle, intelligent, thoughtful, Belle was a woman of great curiosity and much zest for life who was always ready for a new experience, and game to try just about anything. An extremely neat person, as tidy in her appearance as she was in her thinking, I suppose Belle could legitimately have been described as 'frail' — but not by me. She might never have weighed a hundred pounds in her life but, in my view, she was — and is — a human being of unstinting self-reliance, immense inner strength, and indomitable dignity and pride. In a word, "class." That impression was renewed as recently as last summer when Belle and her still-older sister, probably in her early eighties, served my wife and I and one of our sons a superb dinner, featuring vegetables from their own garden, home-baked rolls and pie, and a vast variety of done-down relishes and pickles. At the time Belle retained no more than ten percent vision, and that peripheral, so that she had to look off to one side in order to pick up a plate or knife or fork; but she made not the slightest concession to her infirmity, apologizing only for the fact that, due to short notice, they had had time to prepare only a limited choice of pies and cakes — like two of each. Oh yeah, I like that lady.

But back to the Saturday evening of that Labour Day weekend, just after the war. We had finished our blueberry pie and were sipping our tea or coffee, when somebody else at the table suggested that Belle might like to go fishing.

"Well, that might be fun," Belle conceded, glancing across the table at me. "What do you think, John? I've never caught one. Do you want to help me end my virginity?"

I found myself caught firmly on the horns of a dilemma. On the one hand, I would have done just about anything for Auntie Belle; had she decided that she wanted to be the first woman to land on Mars, I would have at least discussed the arrangements with a travel agent, and might well have gone along to carry her bags and help shepherd her through whatever Customs roadblocks there might be out there in space. On the other hand, I had just put in a positively horrendous week, working fifteen or sixteen hours a day at my summer job with the Manitoba Power Commission, and driving almost all night to get back to the city in time to catch the 'Cottagers' Special' out to Malachi that morning. I was three parts dead; my eyes were hanging down along my cheeks, my heart was pounding and my head was aching like the trip-hammers of hell. If I could have done it without being detected, I would have used toothpicks to prop up my eyelids.

"Why the hesitation?" someone asked, egging me on. "After all, you're supposed to be the resident expert."

I looked out the window. The early September sun was already low, almost touching the tree line to the west, but there was a good hour or more of daylight left. The breeze, fresh but moderate, was curling into the mouth of the bay, and would probably drop off as the twilight began to settle. There was a weedbed across the bay, no more than a five minute run, where catching a walleye was an even surer thing than death and taxes. Hell, I thought, I could get a pickerel for her — her very first fish — and be back at the dock before the dinner dishes were done. Half dead or not, who's going to make a big thing out of boating a routine, co-operative, pound or pound-and-a-half pickerel, for a wonderful woman whom you deeply respect? Not me, said the Little Red Hen.

"Auntie Belle" I responded bravely, if not wisely, "nothing could please me more. Be my guest."

And so, a few minutes later, we walked down to the dock, tiny Belle and I, in the deepening shadows under the big poplars. It was still summer in everything you could see, with no hint of colour in any of the leaves, and the temperature in the soft upper-sixties, and yet there was somehow a hint of fall in the air.

"You'll have to show me what to do," she said, as we got into the boat, an aging Peterborough cedar strip, pushed by a modest outboard motor.

"Don't worry, Auntie Belle," I told her. "It'll be like falling off a log. Fifteen minutes from now you'll have your first fish."

During the short run across the bay, I attached a small, double spoon to the leader on my casting rod. Of all the baits I had tried at Malachi, it was the sure-fire winner for walleyes — a tandem pair of spinners, oval-shaped and a little larger than a dime, followed by a feather-covered, medium-sized set of treble hooks. It had always been an ever-loving, hanging curve ball for walleye fishermen in that lake. Belle sat in the bow seat in her crisp, neatly pressed house-dress, wearing a cardigan sweater to ward off the expected chill of the gathering late summer evening, and looked all around. She has always been one to wring everything she can out of a new experience.

It was only a seven or eight-minute run to the edge of the big weedbed. There are a few cottages rimming the bay, but the shore line of poplars and jack pines is mainly unbroken, and the overall feeling you have as you troll along it is of being in unspoiled wilderness. When we got close, I cut the motor back to trolling speed, picked up my casting rod, and tossed the double spinner behind us, close to the edge of the weeds. I peeled off a few more yards of line, then handed the rod to Belle.

"Hold it like this," I told her, "with your left thumb on the spool of line. If you feel something on it, just holler."

I turned my attention to the motor for a moment. It had not been behaving very well that summer, and you had to fiddle with the needle valve each time to get it running smoothly for trolling. I had had my back turned for a few seconds when I thought I heard Belle say something, but I couldn't make it out over the sound of the motor.

"Pardon?"

"I think I've got something," she said, a little louder.

I figured it was probably a weed, and made a couple of final adjustments to the needle valve.

"Maybe you'd better take it," she said, her voice louder and quavering slightly.

Then I turned around. The rod was bent so that the tip was almost touching the breeze-ruffled surface of the water, and the line stretched out behind us, as taut as a violin string. Belle was hanging on for dear life, her legs tucked under the front seat to avoid being pulled over the side. I might have thought that she was snagged on bottom, except that whatever she was fastened to was moving to the right at a hell of a clip. Oh, God, I thought; that's not your average, friendly, neighbourhood pickerel we've got on there.

"Let me see what I can do," I said, leaning forward and taking the rod from her.

As soon as I felt the sulking, bad-tempered bulk of it, coming through my hands and into my arms, I knew that my first, worst apprehensions had been realized. What had taken the double spinner was not a walleye but a Northern Pike — and a huge one. I had already hauled a twenty-pounder from the lake that summer, but I immediately, almost instinctively, knew that Belle's fish was going to top that with quite a bit to spare.

"You might as well settle back and relax," I said, keeping the line taut as I got to my feet. "We're probably going to be here for some time."

"Is it a big one?" she asked, turning in the front seat so that she could watch the action.

"Not just big, Belle," I told her. "A giant — a real Moby Dick."

"Oh, good" she said.

46

And that brought things squarely to a head. Ordinarily I would have loved to tie into a lunker like that one, but that particular evening, bone-weary and drawn very thin as I was, all I had wanted to do was to help her to boat a small fish as quickly as possible, get back to the cottage, fulfill the minimum social niceties, and hit the sack as early as I decently could. Or earlier. I hadn't bargained on any epic *Old Man and the Sea* endurance contest.

"It's a good one, isn't it, John?" she asked. I had cut the motor by then, and could hear her clearly. And I tried to remember my first fish, a largemouth no doubt, jerked over the gunwale of the white skiff to flap at my mother's feet, but that historic event was shrouded by the mists of time.

"A beauty," I said, "and don't worry — we won't lose him". Not if I could stay on my feet long enough, and my arms didn't fall off, and I didn't permit him those few inches, that moment of slack, which was all he would need to shake the treble hooks from his monstrous, carnivorous, steel-cartilaged jaws.

I had a moment of panic when I realized that we had probably left the gaff hanging in the boat house, but, glancing down, I saw that it was leaning against the back of the middle seat of the boat — *if* I could keep the fish on, and tire it out enough to have a chance to use it.

A lot of people will tell you that a muskie is harder to land than a Northern Pike and, as a generalization, that may be valid, but it's like having to choose between food, drink and sex. Certainly a muskie will come out of the water more, perform more exciting aerobatics, put on a more dramatic show. But I'm inclined to think that a big Northern has more raw, brute strength, and more simple determination. If the muskie is a powerful, run-to-daylight halfback, the Northern is a bulldozing make-a-hole-where-there-is-none, power-your-way-across-the-goal line-fullback. O.J. Simpson versus Larry Csonka.

Belle's fish showed an early tendency to sulk. He continued his run away from the weeds until he decided that he had gone far enough, then just sat on the bottom, six or seven feet beneath the surface, which looked like crinkled lead foil in the oblique rays of the setting sun. Slowly, a few tight turns at a time, I began to ease him in. I had a hundred yards of new, 20 lb.-test nylon line on the reel, and I was confident that I could keep quite a bit of pressure on him — as long as I stayed alert for the unpredictable moment when he would take it into his head to be off again. Not that there was any point in

47

trying to hurry him; I'd known from the start that this fight would go the distance, and I just had to hope that I would still be on my feet to win the decision.

"He's coming," Belle said, almost in a whisper.

"Not for long," I told her, and just then he took off for the foot of the bay. I eased my finger off the spool, and the reel sang as he stripped off line. Fresh as he was, I knew that I couldn't stop him if he decided to simply keep on going, but he inexplicably elected to stop after fifteen or twenty yards. Already my thumb was aching, and there was still a long, long way to go.

Again I began to bring him back — slowly, slowly, a foot at a time. It was three or four runs later before I eased him in close enough for us to have our first look at him. Although he didn't need it, the water magnified his bulk. He looked five or six inches across the back, and as long as you could span with your arms stretched wide. Beyond any doubt, the largest Northern Pike I had ever seen.

"My, oh my," Belle said, kind of reverently.

"Yeah."

"He's so big! A monster!"

"He is that," I concurred, noting that one of the treble hooks was imbedded about halfway back in the lower lip of his huge, menacing, prehensile jaws. I couldn't tell how securely it was set, but the slender curve of tempered steel looked insanely fragile when contrasted against his bulk and strength. We didn't have very long to study him that first time. He saw the boat and took off like a kid's escaped balloon, with the air jetting out of it, back in the general direction of the weedbed.

I stopped him as soon as I dared, and started to work him in towards the boat again.

That sequence set the pattern for the next hour or so. I would crank away at the reel, gaining a few feet of line whenever I could, until I eventually brought him up alongside the boat. He would lie there for a few seconds, in all his great length and might, his broad tail fanning. Resting.

After a while Belle understood the game that was being played out.

"Now?" she would ask.

"Not yet," I would tell her.

And then, in his own good time, the giant fish would take off

48

again, his great head shaking, the power and density of his huge body roiling the darkening grey surface of the bay.

Time passed — fifteen minutes . . . a half-hour . . . longer . . . .

The sun reached the ragged crest of the horizon, touched it, and was swallowed up, as if in quicksand. Instead of going down with it, as I'd expected, the breeze freshened a little with the coming of twilight. In that part of the country you are only a couple of weeks away from frost at the beginning of September, and a chill quickly spread across the water from the shadows of the shoreline. Belle pulled the cardigan more snugly around her shoulders.

We were gradually drifting towards the foot of the bay, the weedbed left a hundred yards behind us. Out near the islands a couple of loons were calling to each other. Three or four flocks of ducks went whistling low over our heads. After a while a three-quarter moon came up, throwing a jagged white path across the water.

By then it seemed that I had been tied to that fish for hours, maybe days. My arms and wrists were bone-weary, my fingers were stiff and sore, and my head ached from lack of sleep the previous week and from the strain of having to concentrate on, and counter, my quarry's every move. Glancing across the bay, I could see the dots of orange light from the coal oil lamps of the cottage, and I thought how marvelous it would feel to be stretched out on the chesterfield in front of the fireplace with a drink near at hand.

I think that, had I been there alone, even though I knew that I was fighting a noble and almost legendary fish, I would have cut the line and let him go. It was not just that I longed for the comforts of the cottage, and resented the demands the big Northern was making on my all but exhausted body. Beyond that, I had come to realize that there was no way in the world that I could realistically ever hope to land him — even if I did eventually tame him to the point where I might try to use the gaff. The simple fact was that I was much too arm-weary to lift that huge body over the gunwale and into the boat. So why keep on with it — a struggle that couldn't be won?

Yet it *was* Belle's first fish, quite probably the only one she would ever hook. And, huddled up against the chill in her inadequate sweater, uncomplaining, engrossed in the classic nature of the struggle, she did not deserve to have it end with the severed end of the line hanging limply in the moonlight. I would have to try to boat it simply because, like the mountain, it was there.

The trouble was that the big Northern showed no real indication of knuckling under. While I was still looking for my second wind, he seemed to be working on his fifth or sixth. The runs were just as long and vicious, the power that came back to me through the line seemed just as intimidating.

"Do you think he's beginning to act a little tired?" Belle asked in what seemed a half-whisper in the moonlight.

"I am, but I don't think he is," I told her.

Another quarter of an hour later we had drifted almost to the end of the bay. It is sandy there, shelving out gradually, with thick stands of rushes on either side. A whip-poor-will was calling a little way down the creek which drains out of the lake at that point.

And then, for the first time, I received an indication that the big fish might be as mortal as I. When I brought him alongside the boat for the twentieth or thirtieth time, I caught a glimpse of his long, pale underbelly in the moonlight. He recovered quickly, but the tell-tale sign had been revealed. His next run was not as long, not as strong, and I turned him with relative ease, the huge head coming around almost submissively. That time I could see a lot of white beneath the dark, moon-spangled surface of the water. There remained the threat of one final, gallant dash for freedom, but to all practical purposes he was subdued. Yet I didn't have the strength to lift him into the boat. He couldn't win, and neither could I; we were like two heavyweights in the final round of a championship fight, each too arm-weary to knock the other out.

"Belle," I asked, "are you too cold to move?"

"Of course not," she said. "What can I do to help?"

"There should be a paddle in the bottom of the boat," I told her.

She groped around for a few seconds in the moonlight.

"I've got it," she said.

"See if you can get us a little closer in to the beach." I didn't realize it then, but I was speaking softly, as if my voice might frighten the fish.

She leaned over and began to use the paddle, willingly, if not very skillfully.

"Nice and easy," I told her, keeping an eye on him. He was drifting beside us then, almost at the surface, belly-up, gills working, the wide orange-tinged tail waving feebly. I didn't think there was any fight left in him, but you can never take a Northern for granted, any more than you can assume the domesticity of a bull.

After a couple of minutes the propellor of the outboard grated lightly on the sand, which would make it about three-and-a-half feet deep at that point.

"You did just fine," I told her. "Now I want you to come back here, and hold the rod for a minute or two."

"All right," Belle said, "but I don't really think I can land him."

"You won't have to," I told her, smiling to myself in the moonlight. "Just keep the rod steady, that's all."

When she had hold of it, I eased myself over the transom, making as little noise and commotion as possible. The water came half-way up my thighs, and felt warm after the chilly night air.

I worked my way carefully around the stern of the boat. The big fish tried to right himself, desperately wanting to make one last rush for freedom. The tail kicked a couple of times, and the big fins worked hard, but he just didn't have enough strength left in him. I could see the wire leader in the moonlight, and I grasped it firmly and waded in towards the beach. He came along docilely behind me, like a dog on a leash whose spirit has been broken.

I reached the edge of the beach, the water squishing in my shoes, and pulled him up onto the clean, dry sand. Knowing that the battle was over, he made no further struggle, but just lay there on his side with his huge jaws opening and closing spasmodically. He was a beautiful fish — clean, with bold markings, deep through the girth, powerfully and almost majestically proportioned. He would go close to thirty pounds, I knew, and nobody was going to take a better fish out of that lake for a long, long time. Yet I felt no sense of conquest, only one of kinship, of shared experience. The big fish and I had gone all the way together, and nobody had really won, nobody really lost.

I stood looking down at him for a minute or so, and then I waded back out to pull the boat in. Belle was standing up in the stern, looking towards the beach, and, inexperienced as she was, I knew that she had a deep appreciation for the moment, and that we would talk about the whole experience, she and I, many times in the future.

The whip-poor-will was still calling, and the moonlight rippled across the bay behind her; the cool breeze coming down the lake made me think that it might be kind of nice to start something going in the fireplace when we got back to the cottage.

"Come on, Belle," I said, taking the bow rope in my stiff, half-numbed fingers, "let's go in and see your fish."

8.
Remember the Time We Shot the Northern Pike?

You'll never hear any argument on behalf of penurious poverty over plush plenty from me, but one of the very best weeks I ever spent — and certainly one of the zaniest — came at a time when my financial tides were at their all-time lowest ebb, which is to say that there was a lot of exposed beach, indeed.

It was 1950 and I was trying to keep my wife, infant son, and I more or less fed, more or less clothed, and more or less sheltered, while I struggled to complete a B.A. from United College in Winnipeg, then an affiliate of the University of Manitoba. The academic part of it was great; I was taking Honors in history and, with Stewart Reid, Trygvie Oleson, Ken McNaught, and Harry Crowe, the History Department at little United College was, man for man, as good as you would find anywhere in North America.

Keeping body and soul together — making ends, if not meet, at least occasionally come within hailing distance of each other — was something else again. The Veterans' Allowance contributed some ninety dollars a month, which was just about enough to keep the temperature above freezing in the winter months — *if* you were lucky enough to have four walls and a ceiling with which to enclose a thermometer.

My best friend during those years was a fellow history major named Gerry. Not quite old enough to have been caught up in the 1939-1945 war, Gerry was constructed along the general lines of a refrigerator — rather square at the corners, broad-shouldered and thick-bodied, but without an ounce of surplus fat. With his short-cropped hair, conservative dress featuring T-shirts and windbreakers, and daily paper bag of sandwiches, he looked like a reactionary, red-necked linebacker on a Texas football team, but thought like an Honour Roll liberal from the Ivy league. Not that he was a political activist on campus for, as he said once or twice, the only thing he had ever joined was the human race. He was too fiercely, although passively, independent to belong to anything, and had too much sense of humor to become involved with movements. His was a whimsical sense of humor; often when you called him on the phone he would answer with "It is I," which would have sounded insufferably corny from some people but was natural and right the way he said it. Perhaps the main thing about him was that, although he understood better than most people how imperfect life is, the awareness never inhibited his ability to enjoy every minute of it. He had a wonderful ability to take things as they come, and, like Auntie Belle, an appealing open receptiveness for anything new — sounds, sights, smells, tastes, experiences, ideas, knowledge.

Like me, Gerry had been born with a tin spoon in his mouth, and we both had to hustle every available moment in order to stay in school — he to pay all of the costs of a university education, me to supplement the meager allowance which the Department of Veterans' Affairs decreed in its wisdom to be sufficient for a student with an embryo family. As a result, when we weren't in school, we worked — on Saturdays, during mid-term school breaks, and from final exams, each late spring, to registration day, each early fall. To stay afloat we worked in the back room of a fruit and vegetable store, fighting off the rats with one hand while we trimmed cabbages, lettuce, and other imported delicacies for the table with the other; manicured golf course greens; cut lawns; hawked magazine subscriptions, home freezer plans, and burial plots — "the marble in this Garden of Remembrance is especially imported from Italy"; trundled wheelbarrows on construction sites; drove trucks; did whatever we had to do to make a buck. One Christmas we both worked in a local haberdashery, selling shirts, ties, socks and pajamas, pressing the pants to our only suits under our mattresses each night. Whoever bought the ties for that store must have been a nearly blind, tasteless and miserable individual who hated all mankind; we had in stock about a hundred identical pieces of neckware patterned in the most hideous confluence of violet, lime green, and orange imaginable, to be outdone perhaps only by the Marquis de Sade. Gerry cooked up a contest in which each salesman, regular or temporary Christmas help, would kick in fifty cents to the confrere who succeeded in selling one of those monstrosities. Our mutual conduct in that affair was disgraceful; we would all assure doting grandmothers, harassed by the exigencies of constricting Christmas shopping time, that the abortion would perfectly complement a blue suit, a brown suit, a grey suit, any kind of sports jacket, whatever the prospective recipient usually wore. The truth was that that tie wouldn't go with anything in anybody's wardrobe, with the possible exception of a peacock's. Gerry didn't win that contest, nor did I, but he had a great time organizing it and we all had a lot of laughs.

As a consequence of all this, by the dawn of our final year at University, neither Gerry nor I had had more than an occasional long weekend off from work and school in almost four years, and so, when my father-in-law suggested that the two of us might like to do some fishing and hunting at the cottage for a week or ten days, and offered to throw in our train tickets to boot, it didn't take us long to accept, especially since my wife, who was able to spend the summers at the lake, gave the idea her endorsement. Nowadays, when college kids feel the need of a break, they take off for Yugoslavia or Acapulco or Katmandu at the drop of a parental check or a government subsidy; as for Gerry and I, we couldn't have been more excited had we been booked for an around-the-world cruise on the *Queen Mary*. For Gerry, the fact that he had always been a city cat, knew nothing about the wilderness, and until then had never held a fishing rod or shotgun in his hands, only added to his sense of anticipation.

As it turned out, he was left to assemble the few supplies our drastically limited budget would permit, following the general guidelines we had worked out a week or two earlier. Typically, I had to work the day of our departure, finishing off my summer job with the Manitoba Power Commission in Brandon, half-way across the province, and (hopefully) getting back to Winnipeg just in time to call for Gerry, get to the railway station, and catch our early evening train to the lake.

For a variety of reasons I didn't arrive at his house until a half-hour before train time, much too late to make the station by public transportation. Fortunately I'd been paid that day, so we called a cab — an extravagance, but, under the circumstances, an unavoidable one.

The cab driver who knocked at the door a few minutes later was tall, thin, sad-looking. We explained that we only had fifteen minutes to catch our train. He told us he didn't think it could be done, but that he'd give it his best shot. The ensuing ride was wild. We ran amber lights, cut through back alleys, ignored the speed limit, and even went a block the wrong way on a one-way street — and made it with three or four minutes to spare.

Having tipped the driver as handsomely as we could afford, we ran into the station, struggling under our loads of miscellaneous baggage.

The first thing we saw on the 'Arrivals and Departures' board in the rotunda was that our train, No. 2, 'The Transcontinental,' was running just over two hours late, and would leave at 9:20.

That left us in a considerable quandry; what to do while we waited out the delay? The idea of sitting around the station for two hours held no great appeal. There wasn't quite enough time to go uptown and take in a movie. Since neither of us had had much to eat since noon, we finally decided to take a bus back to his place and make some supper. Having arrived there, we doddled around, fussed over the food; the whole emphasis was on somehow putting in the long waiting period.

And then Gerry said: "My God, it's almost nine!"

Another frantic phone call to the taxi company. A few minutes later, another knock on Gerry's door. When we opened it, it was the same lanky, cadaverous, sorrowful-countenanced cab driver.

"Don't tell me," he said, resignedly. "I know. You've got fifteen minutes to make the train station. Right?"

"You've got it," we told him.

And so, an instant replay of amber lights, back lanes, one-way streets, the whole bit. This time we got there with six minutes to go before the announced departure time. Well, practice makes perfect. And this time the train jerked and creaked and groaned out of the station on (revised) schedule.

Taking the eastbound Transcontinental out of Winnipeg is always an experience, today as well as in the late forties, because you share it with as heterogeneous a collection of fellow passengers as you are likely to find, except maybe on the Orient Express — nuns, prospectors, Indians, poets, drummers, fishermen, trappers, co-eds, drifters, drunks, cops, robbers, farmers, and business executives who believe that, if man had been intended to fly, God would have equipped us all with wings. Very dry martinis and buck-fifty cigars and the *Financial Post* and *Wall Street Journal* in the bar car; cheap wine drunk out of conical, railway cups, pungent socks, orange peels, the *Ladies' Home Journal* and comic books, and the smell of garlic, in the day coach just ahead.

Gerry and I shared a bottle of cheap rye with a jolly, red-faced priest and a stoical, expressionless Ukrainian storekeeper until they both got off at the little town of Elma, which is about half-way between Malchi and Winnipeg, just where the prairie begins to erupt into the quartz and granite outcroppings of the Great Shield. Old men and women shifted their cramped and creaky bones, and children cried out against the restrictiveness as the train thundered on. After a while we played a few hands of bridge with a white-haired dentist and his wife who had spent many years in the employ of the provincial Department of Health, moving endlessly across the north country in a caboose converted into a dentist's office and living quarters, filling and pulling the teeth of old and young, Indians and whites, prospectors, trappers, priests, surveyors, men and women, drifters, section hands and forest rangers — all that heterogeneous coterie of individuals who exist on the frontier of civilization, and beyond. The dentist's car would stay on some siding, perhaps by the margin of a lonely lake or hemmed in by a fringe of jackpines and poplars, then be hitched onto the end of a freight to be moved a few miles to another way station much like the last.

"Used to get out three weeks every year," the white-haired man said, "not that we were ever that anxious."

"We'd mostly go down to Montreal," his wife said. "First two or three days we'd just look — real yokels, you know? Then we'd start counting the days until we could back."

"What was it you liked so much about the north?" Gerry asked.

"Oh, I don't know," the dentist said. "The people, I suppose. See, down in the cities everybody's trying to put on a show, pretending to be something they aren't. Up here, you don't have to prove anything; just the simple fact of surviving says you belong."

56

"And the fishing," his wife added.

"That, too," the man said, smiling his appreciation. "Why, I've fished lakes and rivers that probably never had a lure in them before."

For the next little while we forgot about the cards, while he and his wife told us about some of their fishing experiences. They said they knew of a pair of wilderness lakes, joined by a short neck of water, where you could stand on a particular point and catch big muskies by casting to your left, huge pike by casting to your right. They talked of a stream where the speckled trout *averaged* close to three pounds, and would hit almost anything you threw into the water. They remembered a time when a huge 'lunge bit clear through a man's finger, an hour after it was supposed to be dead. Outside the train windows the blackness slid past, broken only occasionally by the few scattered, lonely-looking lights of tiny settlements clustered beside the right of way — Brereton, Craig Siding, Winnitoba.

And then we were swinging around the long curve past Copeland's Landing, iron wheels grinding, and slowing for Malachi. Gerry and I, wrestling with our luggage and supplies, and helped by the trainman, got down onto the cinders of the station platform. The great train paused for only a few, impatient seconds, then was gone, hurtling on into the night. I looked around. It was close to midnight by that time. Across the tracks, Simpson's store was in darkness. So was the Forest Ranger's station. So was the Section Agent's house. Or I should say I *surmised* that they were all in darkness. I couldn't really tell. The reason I couldn't tell was that the otherwise completely familiar scene was cloaked in an impenetrable and totally unfamiliar fog.

I didn't want to alarm Gerry, who was trustingly and enthusiastically crossing the threshold into an utterly alien world, but the truth was that I couldn't even see the single light bulb which I was sure would be burning at the end of the Malachi dock.

"Well, might as well get across," I said bravely. "Some onion sandwiches would go pretty good, right?"

"Oh, yeah," Gerry said.

I led the way, with more confidence than I felt, down the slope towards the lake. The dock was there. So was the single, bare light bulb. So was the sixteen foot, cedar strip boat, with the 7½ h.p. motor, my father-in-law had left there for us a month earlier.

We peeled back the canvas cover, loaded our supplies on board, got in. In response to my instructions, Gerry untied the bow rope, while I freed the stern.

"Just a twenty-minute run," I said, in what I hoped was a confident tone. If I'd been using my head at all, we would, of course, have stayed right where we were; the Simpsons, who ran the store would have been glad to put us up, or we could have settled for a slightly uncomfortable, but safe, night in the waiting room of the railway station. To set out across the lake, on the other hand, was an act of lunacy, by which we would almost certainly get hopelessly lost — and could quite conceivably get drowned. None of the cottages would be occupied at that time of year, so there'd be nobody to help us if we got into trouble out there in the fog. Still, the thought of getting to the cottage, and settling in for the start of our long awaited vacation, was highly appealing . . . .

By the time we were a hundred or so feet out from the station dock the debate I was holding with myself had become entirely academic, the single light bulb having already faded out of sight in the fog and inky blackness astern, leaving just the steady drone of the outboard motor and the dank touch of the cloying mist on my face.

It was about two miles to the cottage. The first half of the trip was approximately north, until the long arm of Bradley's Bay was cleared, then an almost ninety degree turn and cut across the mouth of the bay to the cottage. Running at half speed as we were, it should take about twenty minutes before we came abreast of the point-
. . . but I soon decided that such calculations were meaningless. If I tried to think my way through the fog, God knew where we would wind up; the only chance was to do what *felt* right, to act as much as possible by instinct, and hope that memory would serve where conscious mind could not.

Every once in a while I would flick on the flashlight, but it was next to useless — the beam dying two or three boat-lengths away in the gloom, sufficing only to provide an occasional glimpse of Gerry, huddled quietly in the bow. I had no way of knowing what was going on in his mind — communication being impossible over the noise of the motor — but it didn't take much perception to realize that it must have been a traumatic experience for him. Not that he was the type to complain, or that I could have heard any complaints, or that there was anything in the world I could have honestly said to reassure him; but to be out there in the middle of a lake he had never seen, miles and miles from anywhere, on a black September night, in a fog as thick as whipped cream on a pumpkin pie, must have made him wonder what special kind of lunacy had ever beguiled him into setting off into the wilderness with me. An excellent question, to which I had no adequate answer. All I could do was try to retain some blind confidence in my ability to pull us through, and pray a lot.

When my left wrist told me it was time, I pulled the handle over to make the turn around the point. I remember thinking how crazy it was, since I didn't have the faintest idea where we were on the lake. It seemed as if the cottage *should* be up there ahead of us, but we could just as easily have turned completely around and be approaching the station again, or be over by Copeland's on the opposite shore, or be about to pile up on a shoal or on one of the islands . . . .

Finally, my sixth sense suggested that we might be in front of the cottage, in the ludicrously unlikely event that we had been travelling in the right direction on each leg of the trip, and had somehow made the turn at precisely the correct moment. I cut the motor and once more switched on the flashlight.

There was a great mass of rocks and trees no more than thirty or forty feet in front of us. As we drifted closer, and the beam of light feebly penetrated the white/black eternity of the night, I made out the ghostly outlines of a cottage. Not ours. But familiar. The next cottage over. Lane's. By a miracle which, in other circumstances and at a different time, might have got me canonized, we were no more than a long forward pass from our destination.

I started up the motor again and fifteen minutes later we were getting established in the cottage, with the coaloil lamps lit and kindling flames leaping eagerly in the fireplace.

"What I can't understand," Gerry said, shaking his head, "is how the hell you knew where we were out there."

"Sorry," I told him, "but it didn't occur to me you might be worried. Just routine for us old hands."

We slept that night between crisp, lightly-starched sheets and under thick eiderdown quilts which smelled faintly of moth balls.

When we came out into the kitchen the next morning, there was nothing to remind us of the fog except a few wisps of mist dancing over the surface of the bay. There was enough of autumn in the air to make us look forward to the first warmth from the fire we kindled in the wood stove. Outside, a red-headed woodpecker was at work in a pine tree. The bright, mid-September sun was shimmering across the gentle ripples of the lake, which was the delicate blue of a robin's egg, though slightly deeper, slightly more brilliant. The margin of the lake was a wildly zestful, homespun, *Quebecois* sash — yellow poplars and birches, scarlet sumacs, elms of burnished copper, oaks of russet gold, eternally blue/green jackpines. I can still smell that morning's coffee brewing, the rich aroma spiced by a hint of wood smoke; see that morning's toast, browning on the wire rack on the cook stove; hear that morning's bacon, sizzling in the pan.

And thus began an almost ridiculously-perfect, nearly lyrical few days.

To begin with, Gerry had done a great job as our man-in-charge-of-supplies. An atmosphere like that creates prodigious appetites. With almost no experience to fall back on, and an absurdly inadequate budget to work with, Gerry had employed his native shrewdness, spiced by his natural enthusiasm, to ensure that we would eat and drink well, if simply. There were few even slightly indulgent luxuries — no thick steaks, no imported scotch, no jars of caviar.

What we did have were a lot of fine, though sometimes unusual, staples, many of them obtained at bargain prices. For instance, he had discovered a Dutch bakery up on north Main St. which made wonderful, two-foot-long loaves of raisin bread that you could buy at half-price the day after they were baked. Toasted, it didn't matter that the last of the raisin bread was a little stale by the end of our week. And he had an uncle who worked at a packing house which sold smoked pork jowls to its employees at cost, thus providing the finest, thick-sliced bacon I ever tasted. We had the dried peas and onions and other essential ingredients with which to make great, thick, rich, Quebec-style pea soup. We had quite a few bottles of a fine, ridiculously low-priced loganberry wine, bottled in British Columbia. Plus other staples — coffee, butter, flour, powdered milk, and the like.

And we could, of course, abundantly supplement these city-bought commodities by the fish and game which were all around us, in lavish supply, for the taking — wild ducks, ruffed grouse, spruce partridge, pike, pickerel, even a lush second crop of plump, sweet, late-ripening blueberries back on the ridges.

There was also a very special circumstance which helped to make that week at Malachi an unforgettable, time-out-of-time experience. Preparing to start our final year at United College, Gerry and I were both enthusiastic, committed history students, a fact for which our professors had to bear full responsibility. I don't mean that we were 'sweats' or 'book-worms' or whatever other terms of oppobrium may come to mind as descriptive of pedantic, academic, system-conditioned undergraduates. It was just that we liked what we were doing very much, and were looking forward to another year of discovery as to what our world had been, what it was then, and what it might become in the future.

So we had each taken an armful of books with us to the cottage, not for any such practical purpose as getting a jump on our upcoming course requirements, but just because we wanted to. That, thank God, is what Stewart Reid and Ken McNaught and the other members of the History Department had done for us. It was while we were there that I first discovered both Cheyney's beautifully written *The Dawn of a New Era*, and Tawney's magnificent, brilliant *Religion and the Rise of Capitalism*. Those two books alone would have made it an incredible week, had I read them in an igloo at the North Pole. Now *that* is being rich.

Our days fell into a pattern. Breakfast in the warm, pleasant kitchen — crusty raisin bread toast, thick pork jowl bacon, dark woodfire-brewed coffee. Next a few chores — refilling the coaloil lamps, splitting kindling, bringing in wood for the stove and logs for the fireplace, carrying up pails of water from the lake. More than once there was a touch of ground frost on the already fallen leaves in the early morning.

Then we would be outside until mid-day. Sometimes we walked the trail to the foot of Bradley's Bay, along which we could always count on shooting two or three ruffed grouse or spruce partridge. Once we walked the more rugged trail into the Lake of the Clouds. Another day we explored the large island in the middle of the lake, finding a small pre-historic Indian site, rich with pottery shards and pieces of flint, in the process.

In the early afternoon we would return to the cottage, where we renewed our energy with a couple of beers, and a bowl or two of soup — *Habitant* pea, given zest by a hunk of smoked pork jowl, or a variation of the Scottish game soup called Cockaleekie, made from a partridge carcass plus onions, carrots, and potatoes — and more raisin bread, generously spread with butter.

Later, as the sun began to dip towards the horizon, we would vacate the cottage again. Often we would take the boat and go up to the bullrush-rimmed, crescent-shaped entrance to a second lake, where we would troll for pike and pickerel. We never made a swing around that bay without catching at least one fish. A couple of times we went through the narrows into the second lake, and shot a few mallards and blacks in the gathering twilight, as they came winging in to feed on the kernels of wild rice still clinging to their aquatic plants. Coming back down the lake, with the early darkness beginning to close in around us, we could count on seeing deer on the beach near the mouth of Warburton's Bay. One afternoon we went over to the station to pick up a few supplies at Simpson's store. The station platform was stacked with sacks of wild rice, brought in by the Ojibways and Crees from Ottermere, Pelicanpouch, Cygnet, and other lakes farther north. We heard trains go by at odd hours of the day and night, to remind us that there was still a world out there, but, apart from that visit to the station, we didn't see another human being all week.

The evening meal was our daily gourmet treat, eaten in the warm, yellow glow of the coal oil lamps in the kitchen. Often grouse or partridge; I like to oven-cook them with a couple of strips of bacon across the breast, and a half-apple and a half-onion inside the cavity. A couple of times roasted wild duck. Other nights, breaded and deep-fried fresh fillets of pickerel, or pike steaks. Once a baked cottontail rabbit. Hunks of the raisin bread. Simple vegetables — carrots, cabbage, butternut squash, mashed potatoes. Lots of the full-bodied, loganberry wine. A big pot of rice pudding, which we liked to eat cold — made with the same wild rice which would soon be selling in the United States, particularly south of the Mason-Dixon line, for four or five dollars a half-pound.

Finally, the long evenings, with the logs crackling in the big stone fireplace, stretched out reading the history books that meant so much to us. The coffee pot always on the kitchen stove. Occasionally we would break our reading to discuss some point of view we hadn't come across before. Much later on there would be onion or peanut butter sandwiches, a final glass or two of the wine. And eventually to bed. It didn't matter if it was eleven o'clock, or two, or four in the morning. Who cared?

It was the most perfect combination of fresh air, exercise, natural beauty, peace, wildlife, good food and drink, marvelous companionship, and intellectual stimulation anyone could ever hope to experience.

We spent the last afternoon putting the boat and motor away, fastening the shutters over the cottage windows, and in general getting the place ready for the winter. We didn't do it with much enthusiasm. Our train was due in at Malachi at 8:40 the next morning, and we had arranged to have Jimmy Simpson pick us up a half-hour before that and take us to the station to meet it.

Our final day dawned with brilliant sunshine, the lake a dazzling blue and flat, dead calm. We had our bags ready by the door, and had just put away the last of the breakfast dishes, when we heard Jimmy's motor coming across the mouth of the bay. But when we went down to meet him we were surprised to see that, instead of coming in to the dock, he was circling very slowly some fifty or so yards offshore.

"Darndest thing I ever saw," he called to us over the sound of the motor.

"What?"

"There," he replied, nodding towards the surface of the water.

Then we, too, saw it. A fine Northern Pike, in the twenty to twenty-five pound range, was swimming slowly along the surface, much of its powerful back out of the water. Every few minutes it would submerge, leaving a little swirl behind it, only to re-surface again a few feet away.

Jimmy swung the bow of the boat around and came in alongside the dock.

"Got plenty of time," he said. "Train's forty minutes late."

"What do you suppose that fish is doing?" Gerry asked.

"Beats me," Jimmy said.

"Could be sick," I suggested.

"Maybe," Jimmy replied. "Doubt it though, you know. Not about to go belly-up, the way it looks to me."

We went out in the boat and Jimmy stopped the motor. We could see the big fish plainly in the still, clear water, its eyes mean, its big gills opening and closing, its huge tail fanning, half of it protruding into the air. It swam away from us, dove, came up again.

"I'd sure like to know what's causing it," Jimmy said. "You guys got a fishing rod?"

"They're locked away in the boathouse," Gerry told him.

"Probably wouldn't hit, anyway, condition it's in," Jimmy said. "Guess we'll just have to swallow our curiosity."

"Maybe not," I told him. The barrel and stock of my little, single-shot Cooey .22 rifle was in the kit bag at my feet. It took only a few seconds to assemble it, slip in a cartridge, and cock the hammer.

"You going to shoot it?" Jimmy asked. The idea seemed to appeal to him.

"Why not?" I asked.

I waited until the big fish was stationary, then shot it once through the head just above the water-line. There was a brief explosion of water, and then the pike rolled over and was still, its belly very clean and white in the morning sun. Jimmy paddled over and lifted it into the boat, then glanced at his watch.

"By gee, we'd better get going," he said, "unless you fellas want to miss your train." We had spent a lot more time than we realized, watching the big pike.

The run across the perfectly calm lake to the station took about twenty minutes. By the time we had carried our stuff up to the platform, and put the white flag in its socket on the station wall, we could hear the train whistling for Ottermere, a few miles down the track.

"You be sure and let me know what was doing it," Jimmy said, laying the fish down on the cinders beside our luggage.

"We will, don't worry," we told him.

I did, too, in a letter written a week or so later. What I was to discover, when I cleaned the fish back in the city, was that it had tried to swallow a stringer-sized walleye. But Mr. Pike's beady, bad-tempered eyes had turned out to be considerably larger than its quite substantial stomach — or, more precisely, larger than its throat. The pickerel had become stuck part way down, which apparently had made it impossible for the fish to breathe under water, as nature had intended, and forced it to the surface to get air.

The train — No. 2, the Transcontinental — came rumbling into the station, bell ringing imperiously, steam hissing as it escaped from valves. We said good-bye to Jimmy and scrambled on board. Immediately the train lurched forward, and seconds later was swinging into the long curve by Copeland's.

Unshaven, loaded down with baggage, we caused a lot of eyebrows to raise as we made our way along the aisle of the day coach. And, of course, there was the fish. Gerry was carrying it with two fingers hooked into its gills, the great tail dragging on the floor. Some passengers recoiled when they saw it, and one woman was openly indignant.

But the conductor was a fisherman. He arranged to have it put on ice in the kitchen of the dining car, which meant that the big Northern got to travel first class.

It seemed a fitting ending somehow to the very special saga of that September week.

9.

Walter and I

Walter and I spent a lot of time together in the navy during the war and, unlike most shipmates who swore that they would keep in touch and then never saw each other or communicated in any way again, we did maintain a relationship for many years after the hostilities and indignities were over.

Walter was a guy who wore well. Tall, curly-haired, slightly thick-lipped, he had been a pretty fair trumpet player with some of the top Ontario bands of the pre-war era. He had a wonderfully sardonic sense of humour. "Do you know the only difference between me and Harry James?" he would ask. "Talent, that's all — just miserable, goddamned talent." He liked to think of himself as a pool shark, but Sophie Tucker could have spotted him ten points and taken nine out of ten snooker games from him. Shooting blindfolded. He took an accounting course after the war, and was a hell of a good man with a balance sheet, but he could never take the high finance game seroiously; as a result, he drifted from job to job, always making a good enough living, but unwilling — or perhaps congenitally unable — to go through the profit-and-loss charade with a straight-enough face to ever make it to anyone's board of directors. Which is a large part of why he was such unusually good company.

I don't mean to imply that Walter and I were constant companions; far from it, but we managed to get together on a regular basis three or four times a year. One such annual occasion was our yearly trout-fishing junket.

In Ontario the trout season always opens on the Saturday closest to the first of May. Preceding the walleye season by some two weeks, and the start of muskie and bass fishing by almost sixty days, the trout opening marks the end of six long, impatient months of inactivity for most angling addicts.

Now, to be honest about it, neither of us were exactly Izaak Waltons when it came to catching brook trout. Oh, sure, set us down beside some wilderness lake or stream in the far north or Newfoundland, where the brookies are unsophisticated and hungry, and stacked up like 727's in a holding pattern over Kennedy Airport in a fog, and we'd bring back enough speckles to fill a frying pan. But trout fishing in southern and central Ontario was something else again. Here, within a hundred or so miles of Toronto, generations of brook trout had become wise and wily in the survival process of outwitting the sons and grandsons and great-grandsons of the early eager piscatorial Nimrods. Most of the best trout water had been posted ('PRIVATE PROPERTY — KEEP OUT!'), and the few stretches of streams and lakes that remained open to the public were certain to be lined three-deep, like Bonanza Creek at the dawn of the Klondike gold rush, come opening day.

You had to be both good and lucky to take trout under these circumstances — and Walter and I were neither. In the true spirit of fishermen everywhere, we did not, however, permit such unpleasant realities to dissuade us from continuing to make our annual spring pilgrimages. When we returned home each May — bone-weary, dirty, wet, cold, smelly, empty-creeled — we would say with the determined optimism of the long suffering, but still dedicated, sports fan: "Wait 'till next year!"

We would usually start to make our plans somewhere around the beginning of February. The fire in a fisherman's heart never dies completely, and it didn't take much to set the embers glowing. An unseasonably warm day with a sun bright enough to start the snow melting would do it. Or an article in an outdoor magazine. Or a glimpse of your rod and tackle box when you were rummaging around in the basement, looking for the spare filter for the oil furnace. For an unregenerate fisherman, there is no warmer, more nostalgic, happier event imaginable than a casual encounter with your tackle box some mid-winter night when the hockey game on television has degenerated into a let's-get-it-over-with-and-settle-for-a-two-all-tie farce, and a blizzard is howling beyond the basement windows, and piling snow that will eventually have to be shovelled in drifts across your driveway. You sit down near the fireplace and start to sort and sift through it. There is the big plug with the teeth marks where you damn near hooked that huge muskie back of Gibson's Island the previous July. There is the last of the three leaders you bought at Morley's Bait Shop the Sunday morning of the Civic Holiday weekend. There is the straightened-out hook from the encounter with whatever it was in that little, waterlily-encircled bay. There are the tangled remnants of all the previous summer's dreams. And so you would start to think about another season and, like baseball players in spring training, where everybody is a .300 hitter, you would *know* that all of your past failures had been the product of star-crossed misadventure, rather than a lack of skill. *This* would be the year.

And so, about then one of us would phone the other, and we'd get together for lunch or a couple of drinks after work. After that there might be four of five further meetings as we crossed off the days of February, March and April on our desk calendars with growing impatience. Somehow, as proof that hope does spring eternal in the breast of the real fishing fanatic, we would always come up with some new spot to try that we were unequivocally convinced would produce limit catches of twelve and fourteen-inch trout come opening day. The tips came from all kinds of unlikely sources — a bartender who had overheard a couple of drunks arguing about trout fishing, a car jockey who came from this little town with the stream running through it where you could catch enough fish for supper any day on your way home from school, somebody who knew a doctor whose old spinster sister still had the family farm with a pond on it just teeming with speckles that nobody knew about. Of course, with our largely fishless past record, Walter and I were in no position to throw any kind of a lead back, however dubious the source might be.

And so, through some alchemy of eternally reborn hope and mutual self-deception, we would settle on the destination for that year's safari. St. Eustace Creek, McDermott Lake and Little Cedar River are three names that I remember — mostly because there are things associated with each that I would much prefer to forget.

Then Walter and I would make our annual trek to the government office to buy topograghical maps for whatever area we had selected. It's amazing how you can see trout in every widening of a stream on a one-inch-to-the-half-mile map in a dimly lit bar on an early March night when a blizzard is blowing outside. We always planned our trips with great care — deciding just where we'd park the car, the easiest path into the creek, whether we'd work upstream or down, where we'd stop for lunch, and so on. Compared to us, General Rommel was downright casual in working out his strategy for the battle of El Alemain. One thing I have to say, though — we never did forget the rum, not once in all those years.

The trout season is traditionally rung in at the stroke of twelve on a Friday night. Operating according to our complicated, logistical timetable, Walter and I would drive out of Toronto sometime during the night, the exact hour having been arrived at by weighting various factors, such as the number of miles we had to cover, the probable condition of the roads, our relative optimism, and the degree to which we were willing to countenance heckling from our spouses, other family members and neighbors. The end-product of this equation was always calculated to get us to the selected location just prior to dawn on the Saturday morning. Needless to say, our calculations didn't always work out perfectly. Once we got there at two o'clock in the morning, and had finished the rum long before the first, grey light showed through the bare branches of the trees. Another time we didn't arrive until two in the afternoon — but that turned out to be the wrong creek in the wrong county, anyway.

Let me tell you about a few of our more indelibly-stamped disasters. St. Eustace Creek proved to be a dank, dark, black hole of a cedar swamp — the kind of place where crocodiles would be an endangered species simply because their little minds would tell them that there had to be a better place to live. The mosquitoes loved it, though; Walter went in weighing one sixty-nine, and came out two hours later hitting the scale at close to one-eighty. It was the first time I had ever seen high-rise mosquito bites.

McDermott Lake was where we encounter the bull in the middle of the mile-wide pasture. That was before the old lady who owned the place came out and fired rock salt at us from her trusty, double-barreled .16-gauge shotgun. Must have been a descendant of Daniel

Boone, that venerable crone. Slightly lacerated, we did salvage something from that day, though; when the bull charged, Walter set two world's records simultaneously — for the 237 yard dash, and for the sprawling high jump.

When we got to Little Cedar Creek, the year that it was singled out as our oasis, it was to find it in such a state of flood that even the most intrepid of Mark Twain's side-wheeler captains would have sought sanctuary at some convenient pilings along Old Miss. Walter and I waded in. Cakes of ice, each big enough to sink the *Titanc* or chill Dean Martin's martinis for a year, were drifting by. The only thing anybody might possibly have hoped to catch there was an Artic Grayling.

About an hour after we arrived, Walter glanced over at me, his teeth chattering, his legs braced to avoid being swept away, looking for all the world like Henry Hudson in waders.

"What the hell are we doing here?" he asked.

I couldn't think of an answer.

"One good thing," I said, trying vainly to control my shivering, as we headed back for the car.

"I'd be glad to hear about it," Walter said.

"We should be thankful it wasn't the *Big* Cedar."

"Amen" he said, "wherever the hell *that* is."

But the worst time was the year we headed for a little lake away up in the Ottawa valley. We had decided by then that we'd have to go further afield if we wanted to have any real chance of breaking our string of shutouts. I think it was Walter who came up with that red hot lead. It was kind of tough to get into, his source told him, but the effort was worth it, since the lake was full of trout and hardly ever saw a fisherman.

We studied the topographical maps with particular care that year, concluding finally that we could drive to within a quarter-mile of the lake by following an old logging road for the final short leg of the trip.

The long-awaited Friday night finally came, and we left Toronto about midnight, an hour which an earlier strategy session had determined should get us to the lake a half-hour or so before first light. It was a dreadful night as we headed out of the city — windy, as dark as an abandoned mine shaft, rain driving down in sheets.

"Maybe it'll get better as we head north," Walter said bravely.

But the only thing that changed was that the rain occasionally congealed into wet snow.

A couple of coffee stops had been scheduled along the way, but because of the awful weather we decided that we'd better press on straight through. The expressway gave way to a two-lane strip of black top, after which, consulting our topographical maps by the dome light of the car, we found a county highway, then a gravel road, and finally, almost miraculously, a narrow gap in the trees which identified the beginning of the old lumbering road. I glanced at my watch; it was ten after four in the morning.

"We're gonna have some time to kill," I said.

"Well, better early than late," Walter remarked, without much conviction.

Naturally, the lumbering road turned out to be impassable. A white pine, about three feet through the trunk at the base, had fallen across it some years back. Ten Paul Bunyons couldn't have budged it.

"Anyway, it can't be more than a mile in," Walter said.

It probably wasn't, either, by any kind of a direct route. The way we went, though, stumbling and falling, tripping over deadfalls, barging into trees, groping our way through the rain and black night, it was approximately the distance from Toronto to Vancouver.

Finally we came out on what had to be the lake. We knew that because all of a sudden there was nothing left to bump into. It was still pitch dark, and there didn't seem to be any reason to believe that the sun would ever come up again. Still, we shared the excitement of knowing that out there in the inky blackness were practically virgin waters, just teeming with voracious, naive trout.

"Well, what do you think?" Walter asked, his voice disembodied. I could sense that he was there, two feet away, but I couldn't see him.

"Guess we might as well get started," I told him. "No point in just waiting around, getting soaked." Not that either of us could lay claim to a square inch of dry skin.

We edged our way cautiously down the slope to what we presumed must be the shore of the lake, holding our rods and tackle boxes high, feeling for each next step with largely numbed feet.

"Figure this is about it," Walter said at last.

"Guess so."

"Well, good luck."

"You, too."

We edged apart a few feet to give ourselves room to cast. I was ready first because I had tied on a small double spinner before we left the car. I didn't know how Walter was going to find and attach a lure in that Stygian blackness, but he would have to cope with the challenge as best he might. Usually your eyes adjust to the darkness, at least to some extent, but, ten minutes after we got there, you still couldn't see your hand in front of your face.

"Well, here goes," I told him.

"Yeah — first cast, first fish!" he said, with the confidence that is always reborn during long winters of no fishing.

I swung the rod behind me, then snapped it forward. The season was underway, the long famine over at last. I waited for the little splash as my spinner hit the unseen water. But there was no little splash; there was a little tinkle instead. A faint, tinny, little tinkle.

To make sure, I made a few turns of the reel. There was no drag on the line, just the sense of the spinner skittering along over something flat and hard.

"Walter," I said softly.

"Yeah."

"Don't bother fixing up your line."

"What ?"

"Ice," I told him. "It's still in."

By the time we got back to the car, wet night was grudgingly giving way to wet day, and you could make out ghostly grey shapes in the woods — two of the ghostliest being Walter and I. We spent the morning in the car with the rain pelting down on the roof, as dismal a sound as anyone is likely to hear. Red-eyed, weary, dispirited, cramped, and soaked through, I don't suppose I have ever been more uncomfortable. We turned the car heater on once in a while, but that only changed the chilly dampness into steamy dampness, the smell of our old fishing clothes somehow reminding me of long-ago Sunday school classes on winter afternoons. The rum helped some, and we ate most of what was supposed to have been our lunch. We slept a little off and on, each fitful nap adding another crick or two to necks, shoulders, and backs. The topographical map showed that there were two or three creeks in the area which would probably be open, and might have trout in them, but the rain continued to pour down, and neither of us had the heart to go looking.

Around noon we drove into Smith Falls and spent a good part of the afternoon drinking draft beer in the beverage room of one of the old hotels on the main street. The smart thing, of course, would have been to head for home right away, where hot showers and comfortable beds were a-waiting. But our wives would be waiting, too, and we suffered enough ridicule each May opening without arriving home in the middle of the day with our soaking wet tails between our legs. We had already decided not to say anything about the ice, which is why neither of them ever learned about that particular ignominy until now. Anyway, what fisherman has ever been known to do the smart thing?

The beverage room was filled with locals — district farmers in coveralls, citizens in work clothes, young bucks wearing hockey club windbreakers, here and there a couple of old-timers dragging on their pipes between sips of beer.

"I have a terrible conviction," Walter said, along about the fourth draft.

"About what?" I asked.

"That ten days or so from now, when the weather turns sunny and warm, and the ice is gone, every character in this room is going to go out and get his limit," he said.

"Yeah," I agreed, "in maybe an hour-and-a-half."

A little later a big, red-faced farmer, a middle-aged man with a bulbous nose and an open, friendly face, joined some acquaintances at the table next to ours. After a few minutes he turned towards Walter and leaned over in his chair.

"You fellas wasn't fishin', by any chance?" he asked, glancing at our still damp and rumpled clothes.

"Fishin'?!" Walter said, "In this weather? No, no, we're with the Department of Mines. Doing a little surveying back north a piece. Too wet to work today, though."

"Too wet to do anything except this," the farmer said, lifting his glass. Then he turned back to his companions.

"Walter Crowe been in yet today?" he asked.

"Ain't seen him," somebody answered.

"Tells me a couple of city fellas druv into that lake near his place sometime in the middle of the night," he said. He started to laugh, down deep in his ample belly. "Lookin' for trout, I guess. Dang fools didn't even know the ice ain't out yet." He just managed to contain his hilarity long enough to tell his friends.

"Well, don't that just about beat all?" one of them asked, shaking his head, and slamming his fist down on the table.

The others joined in the merriment. So did the two guys from the Department of Mines at the next table.

You would have thought that the utter defeat and humiliation of that day might well have written *finis* to the continuing saga of our annual opening day trout fishing pilgrimages, but it didn't. The demise came two years later beside a swollen creek, up north of Kaladar.

That was the day we came upon the grotesquely fat lady in the house dress, who was fishing with a fly rod so old that Jacques Cartier might have brought it over as a *bon voyage* gift from his grandfather. A perfect casting choice for the 'Before' half of a reducing plan ad, she didn't even bother with a reel, had just tied a short length of casting line to the rod tip, in somewhat the same manner she might knot a clothesline around a spindly cedar tree. Beside her on the bank there were six or seven plump trout, the best running close to a sixteen inches in length.

As usual, Walter's creel and mine were mockingly empty.

"For my cats," The fat lady told us.

That did it.

10.
The Bass Are Taking Dill Pickles

I used to have a business partner named Harry who only discovered the pleasures to be gained from fishing at a comparatively advanced stage of his life. Someone at whose Muskoka cottage he was staying for the weekend took him out, and he managed to haul in a couple of marginal smallmouths. That was enough to snooker him; Harry became an instant addict. (As a group, fishermen are, of course, far more firmly hooked than any finny quarry they are likely to bring to their landing nets.)

Harry, who tended to run to fat and was hopelessly out of shape, had a typically Torontonian concept of the dimensions of his province. To him, anything beyond the outermost high-rise apartment concept was 'the country,' and anything above Barrie, an hour's drive up Highway 400, was 'the north,' i.e. unspoiled, and virtually unexplored, wilderness.

For some years his fishing experience was limited to easily accessible, basically fished-out, southern Ontario lakes, where the very best you could hope for was a couple of immature walleyes or possibly an occasional smallmouth running to maybe a pound, and where you are never more than a few minutes or so away from a dark cocktail lounge where the bartender knows what is meant by 'a really dry martini.'

Harry was good company, as knowledgeable about many other things as he was naive about fishing, and I often talked to him about some of the catches I had made at Malachi where, I insisted, the pickerel had to fight for swimming room, the bass ran to four and five pounds, and there was more than one Northern Pike with approximately the displacement, and certainly the evil disposition, of a U-boat. I don't know how much of all this Harry believed — it was a little like trying to describe the Louvre to a New Guinea aborigine who has spent his entire life drawing suns on the wall of a cave — but he was intrigued enough to insist that he'd give anything to go there if the opportunity ever presented itself.

The chance finally came via a business conference in Minneapolis one mid-June, to which our company consented to send us — not without considerable persuasion from Harry and I, since both of us had consistently declined to attend other conferences much closer to home and of far clearer relevancy to the marketing and opinion research dodge which provided us all with bread and butter. From Minneapolis it is only a relatively short plane hop to Winnipeg, and from there we could reach Malachi by train in a little over three hours.

We laid our plans during two or three after-work sessions at the office, lightening the strain with the occasional belt of rye and water. Our principal objective was to spend as little time as thorough scheming would permit at the conference, and as much time as possible at the lake. A careful study of the agenda revealed that, although the conference ran from mid-week through Saturday, the only speeches that could conceivably be worth hearing were scheduled for the first afternoon, immediately following registration. We agreed that we should sit in on those talks, but could easily fake attendance for the rest of the week by picking up advance copies of some of the later speeches, reading newspaper accounts, and calling another guy from Toronto who we knew would stay to the bitter end (he being considerably more afaid of his boss than we were of ours) when we got back home.

We flew out of Toronto on an early flight, transferred at Chicago, and arrived in Minneapolis in time for a late lunch, after checking in at the hotel which was the headquarters for the convention, registering, and receiving the silly name tags which seem to be *de rigueur* at all such functions. The speeches were dull and riddled with platitudes, but we found a fine German restaurant for dinner, and later a comfortable bar where we put in a pleasant evening. Then a noon flight to Winnipeg the next day on an antiquated aircraft that landed at

Fargo, Minot, Bismarck and one or two other North Dakota points, and flew at about six thousand feet, gamboling happily with the hot air currents rising from the prairie, which tossed us around like a ping pong ball in a laundry drier. Our train didn't leave for a few hours, which gave our stomachs time to settle back out of our throats and into their more-or-less normal positions, and it was early evening before we reached the lake and took the boat across to the cottage. It was a little too late to go fishing that evening, so we settled for a pitcher of martinis and a couple of thick steaks, went to bed early, and slept the sleep of two blessed escapees from the Minneapolis convention.

The next morning, after an appropriate northwoods breakfast, we set out up the lake in the cedar strip boat, pushed by a 7½ h.p. outboard motor. It is hard to imagine anything more beautiful than the lake was that morning. The cottages, stretching out for some distance from the station, were soon behind us, and the margin of the lake ahead and on both sides of us was unbroken wilderness. The sun seemed to twinkle in a cloudless sky. The water, its surface barely broken by the slightest of breezes, was a brilliant, vibrant blue. The poplars and birches, poking out between the ragged, dark spires of the jackpines, were incredibly delicate and fresh-looking in their recently mature foliage.

Back in Toronto I had made what must have seemed like crazy forecast, pinpointing the precise moment and place where Harry would get his first strike. I had drawn a map on a scratch pad in Harry's office, identifying the main features of the shoreline, and pointing out in particular an ancient, silvery, pine stump with twisted roots, which rested on a little beach just inside the point of the third bay we would come to.

"When we go past that stump," I had told him, with the assurance that is lent by time and distance on such occasions, "you'll get a strike. Most likely a Northern Pike. Say about six or seven pounds."

The look on Harry's round face had clearly reflected his skepticism when I made that prediction; it was one thing to boast about the fishing in the lake, but another to call the shot exactly as if I had written the script in co-operation with the fish. As a matter of fact, I wasn't really taking as big a chance as it seemed. I couldn't remember going by that stump more than two or three times without getting a strike of some kind. Oh, maybe it *was* a little chauvinistic to go so far out on a limb as to specify the weight, but I was pretty sure he'd tie into something with fins before we finished our pass along that little beach.

Then we were coming around the point of the third bay on the way up to the head of the lake, and there was the twisted old stump, just as I had described it to him a month earlier and fifteen hundred miles away. And I had the sinking feeling that this would be the time when the law of averages would catch up with me, and I would surely regret having been such a show-off. I cut the motor to trolling speed, and Harry cast out his lure — a double spinner with feathered hooks, as I had recommended. It wasn't a very good cast, but the spoon waddled out about fifty feet before plopping into the water. The line grew taught as it swung around astern of the boat. And then, at the exact moment we drew abreast of the stump, the tip of his rod jerked sharply a couple of times and bent and throbbed under the weight of a fish.

"Got one!" Harry exulted.

"Sure," I said, feigning surprise that he had ever doubted my integrity, "just like I told you, right?"

It turned out to be a modest little Northern, six or seven pounds (the god who watches over loudmouths was smiling on me that day), but it was the biggest fish Harry had ever landed. He was decimated when I disengaged the hooks carefully and returned the pike to the lake.

"What did you do that for?" he asked.

"No sweat," I said. "There'll be plenty more."

And there were, of course. You can catch fish there almost any time, but early June is Old Home Week for walleyes and, as for the Northerns, they seem to spend the whole of their lives just waiting to hit something. The bass are plentiful there, too, and they run large, but the season for them wouldn't open for another couple of weeks.

We trolled a good part of the shoreline, catching walleyes almost as fast as we could get our lines out and crank them back in again. We must have boated forty or fifty of them, the majority around two to three pounds, all of which we returned to the water. We would save a few for dinner later on, but that could wait until we were ready to head back to the cottage. There were a few northerns for variety, too, a couple of them in the twelve to fifteen-pound range.

Harry was having the time of his life. He had never seen anything like it, and was like a kid under the tree on Christmas morning. He had brought along an 8 mm movie camera, and we took some film of each other bringing in the fish. I got one shot that he really liked, of him throwing two good sized walleyes back into the lake, one with each hand.

"So they'll believe it back home," he said.

Later in the morning we eased our way through a weed-lined narrows into another body of water, unimaginatively described on the topographical map as 'Second Lake.' You had to tilt the motor up and use the paddles to get over a couple of shallow spots in the short passage between the lakes, and when we got there a big bull moose was standing up to its knees in the water, eating the young lily pads. Harry had never seen one before, and he was amazed — and a little alarmed — at its immense proportions. The moose seemed none too pleased to see us, and for a moment I thought he might have it in mind to challenge us for the right of way. But he finally turned — more in disgust than in anger, it appeared — and ambled noisily into the bush, knocking down a couple of small dead trees that hppened to be in his path.

As was usually the case, the fishing was even better in the second lake, and by noon we were both not only ravenously hungry but ready for a rest. We pulled the bow of the boat up on the shelving rock of the point of an island, and had our lunch, reclining on a thick carpet of brown leaves.

It was an incredibly beautiful day — cloudless sky, just a light breeze coming up the lake, the sun pleasantly, lazily warm. Only the occasional cawing of a crow disturbed the peace and solitude.

As we finished the coffee from the thermos jug Harry was sitting with his back to the water, while I was facing the lake. The remnants of our lunch were spread between us. We both had a powerful sense of richness, of being blessed, of immense well-being.

"I never thought I'd see fishing like this," Harry said.

"Yeah, it's something, allright," I agreed.

"I'd sure like to give the bass a try some time," he said.

"You want a bass?"

"Sure, but it's out of season."

"You wouldn't have to keep it," I told him.

"That's true."

The fact was that, while we were talking, I had been looking past Harry to where a big male bass, probably four pounds or more, was hovering in the shallow water over the sand at the edge of the rock shelf where we had pulled up the boat. It being spawning time (which was why the season would not open until the end of the month), the bass was guarding the nest previously prepared by his mate. Having fulfilled her function, the female had departed by then, but the male would stay there until the fry had sufficiently developed to disperse and fend for themselves. During all of that time, a period of a couple of weeks or more, he would not leave, even to search for food. And I knew from past experience that he would immediately attack anything entering the area of the nest — be it a big pike, a turtle, or a stick or stone thrown into the water — whether from hunger, anger, frustration, or an instinct for protecting his progeny, I don't know.

Harry was still almost totally naive about the ways of fish, and I couldn't resist trying to take advantage of the situation. He, of course, had no idea that the big bass was there, just a few feet behind him.

"I'll bet there are bass just off the point there," I said.

"You think so?"

"Sure."

"Maybe I'll take a few casts just for the heck of it," he said, reaching for his fishing rod.

"Uh-uh" I said, "I don't think that will work."

"Why not?"

"Got to still fish for them this time of year."

"I didn't know that."

"Yeah, lazy as hell in June. Won't chase anything. Got to drop it right in front of them."

"Well, that settles that," he said, putting the rod back down again.

"Why?"

He spread his hands. "No live bait," he said.

"Oh, we ought to be able to think of something," I told him.

"Like what?"

I glanced around at the remnants of our lunch, hoping to come up with something truly memorable, really outlandish. A piece of hard-boiled egg — too soft to stay on the hook. A bit of crust from a ham sandwich — too prosaic. A piece of old cheese — too crumbly, and besides I liked old cheese. A banana peel — not bad, but still I wasn't quite satisfied. Then my eyes fastened on the perfect prop.

I picked up a jar, and handed it to Harry.

"Here, try one of these."

He looked at me incredulously.

"What are you giving me? A dill pickle! Oh, come on! That's silly."

It was my turn to show surprise.

"You never heard of using dill pickles for bass?"

"Sure as hell, I didn't," he said.

"You think gherkins are better?" I asked him. "Some people do."

"I'm just not into pickles of any kind for fishing. That's crazy."

"I guess it does sound a little weird at that," I said. "Too bad Mr. Simpson isn't here — he'd tell you."

"Who's Mr. Simpson?"

"Runs the store over at the station. Been on this lake fifty years or more. Might have been him who discovered it, for all I know."

"Dill pickles?"

"Yeah."

"For bass?"

"Yeah, that's what I'm telling you. He stocks them by the case over in the store. Indians won't use anything else, and they've got to catch fish to eat."

"Oh, come on," Harry said, but it seemed to me that he was beginning to waver a little.

"Do those have garlic in them?" I asked.

He picked up the jar, and looked at the label.

"Yeah, it says 'with garlic.'"

"That's good. They seem to work best."

I was trying to imagine old Jacob, an Ojibway I knew, setting out in his canoe to catch supper for his family with a jar of kosher dills propped up against the ribs in front of him. It wasn't easy to hold back the laughter.

"You really think they'll work?" Harry asked.

"Have I ever lied to you before?" I countered. "What about the stump? Just like I told you it would be — right?"

"Well, yeah."

"Then why not give it a try?"

"What would make a bass want to eat a dill pickle?" he asked, still not convinced.

"Why not? You like them, don't you?"

"Sure, but I'm not a bass."

"Maybe it looks like a frog to them in the water," I said. "All I know is it'll work, believe me."

"All right" he shrugged. "There's a first time for everything."

"That's the spirit."

He unsnapped his leader, replaced the double spinner he had been using for trolling with a single, still-fishing hook, and imbedded the barb carefully in one of the dill pickles, after fishing it out of the liquid in the jar with his thumb and index finger. The smell of garlic was pretty zesty, and the thought crossed my mind that dills might work pretty well for catfish. I'd have to try them sometime.

Harry went the few feet out onto the point, shaking his head.

"I still think this is crazy," he said.

"That's what they told the Wright brothers, but we flew out to Minneapolis, didn't we? Just throw it out to your right there, about ten or twelve feet. That looks like a good spot to me."

He stripped off some line, and tossed the 'bait' out into the water. It landed with the sort of 'plunk' you would expect of a dill pickle.

Perfect — just a couple of feet to one side of the nest-guarding bass. Almost the instant it touched the surface there was a kind of explosion from underneath as Big Daddy came charging up to the attack. His momentum took him clear out of the water, so that Harry got a good look at what he had tied into. Better than four pounds, I thought, and with part of the dill sticking out of his pugnacious jaws.

"My God!" Harry had time to say.

As it turned out, we didn't have to release the out-of-season bass after all, because Harry didn't catch it. The fish made one ferocious run, and then spit out the hook when he came out of the water for the second time.

That old mossback would have been hard enough to land at any time, but he seemed to be in a particularly foul mood that June day. You couldn't blame him. His wife had run off and left him. He had to stay there, day after day, while the fry gradually developed. He was half-starved.

And no doubt he had never developed a taste for dill pickles.

11.
May Days at Lake Nipissing

One of the best places I know of in which to open the pickerel season is North Bay, Ontario — partly because the fishing is usually superb, and partly because the atmosphere there in the middle of May is unique.

North Bay is on the northeast corner of Lake Nipissing, some two hundred and twenty-five miles north of Toronto. Linked by the French River to Georgian Bay to the southwest, and by Trout Lake and the Mattawa to the Ottawa River in the east, Lake Nipissing was once an important part of the historic route of the fur traders and explorers from Quebec City and Montreal to the West. It is a very large body of water and, in any other part of the world, where it would not have the Great Lakes to provide a comparison, it would be regarded as an inland sea.

On the southeastern fringe of the city of North Bay there is a large, horseshoe-shaped extension which represents the eastern head of the giant lake. It is called Callander Bay after the small town which nestles on its shores, the birthplace of the famous Dionne quintuplets, who first saw the light of day there in the early 1930's. The northwestern arm of that bay is known locally as Sunset Point.

Travelling by car, you can bypass North Bay, or you can go into the city by Highway 11B, which skirts the end of Lake Nipissing and takes you along a two or three mile stretch of cheek-by-jowl motels, cottages, and overnight tourist cabins. Most have boats and motors for rent, sell bait and other fishing supplies, and welcome the extra revenue provided by the early season invasion. I have never been there in July or August but can imagine that it might be a pretty claustrophobic spot in which to spend even one night at the peak of the summer tourist period, surrounded by bawling kids and distraught, behind-schedule parents, trying to make it to Saskatoon and back during their annual two or three week vacation.

In mid-May, however, on the weekend on which it becomes legal to catch pickerel (and Northern Pike), the lakeside establishments are solidly booked by dyed-in-the-wool fishermen from southern Ontario, Michigan, Ohio, New York, and other widely dispersed bailiwicks. Because they are all there for a single primary purpose (to catch fish), a spirit of boisterous camaraderie prevails. Women's lib notwithstanding, it is an almost exclusively masculine weekend, characterized by enthusiastic drinking, late night poker-playing, hard core profanity, practical jokes, and other, more or less juvenile hijinks.

Come opening morning, an incredible number of boats will be anchored out on the lake — as many as a hundred or more clustered off Sunset Point, numerous others grouped in various parts of Callander Bay and towards North Bay, in the opposite direction. Most of the fishing is done in from thirty to fifty feet of water, and almost everybody uses live minnows for bait. It is rare to see a boat out there at the beginning of the season that doesn't have at least a couple of fish, and a majority usually wind up with full stringers. The walleyes don't run particularly large, averaging perhaps around two pounds, but there is always the possibility of tying into a good pike to add variety and zest to the proceedings.

One interesting aspect of fishing there at that time of year is the extraordinary range of temperatures which may be encountered from year to year, and even from day to day. I have been there when the big lake was like a mill pond, and the sun so hot that everybody had their shirts off and the nearby drug store was sold out of sun tan lotion by mid-afternoon. I have also sat out on the lake in a blinding snow storm, huddled deep in a parka, gloved hand half numb on the handle of my fishing rod, my thermos of hot coffee spiked with rum and the stubborn stupidity familiar to all fishermen the only things keeping me from going in and returning to my warm bed.

The wind is an ever-present danger on that immense lake. It can come up without warning, transforming lulling calm into angry, raging sea in a matter of minutes. It can swing completely around, as if at the flick of a switch, changing from a gentle, off-shore breeze into a driving gale before you have time to ponder how long a run it is to the nearest shelter.

We learned all about that wind one afternoon a few years back.

Four or five of us from the same office used to go up there every opening weekend. We'd leave Toronto as early on the Friday afternoon as we could get away, arrive at North Bay sometime in the evening, fish most of Saturday and Sunday morning, and drive back to the city in time to have dinner with our families.

The others were excellent company, good drinking and poker companions, and they could catch their share of fish in those supersaturated waters. But I was the only one of the group who had had any real experience with boats. As long as we stayed close to Sunset Point, a five-minute run from our motel dock, that didn't matter much. But Frank, who had introduced our group to the joys of opening the walleye season on Lake Nipissing, had a strong, almost compulsive hankering to go out to "the islands." A Toronto neighbor had taken him to North Bay the year before he talked us into trying it, and the two of them had made the trip out there, where they had run into some fabulous fishing — the walleyes running to five and six pounds. It was natural that Frank would want to give it another shot. The others in our group were more than willing to go along — all, that is, except me.

The trouble was that the islands in question are quite a long way out in the lake, across four or five miles of open water from the North Bay shore. Low lying, they are not much more than visible on the distant horizon from our usual fishing grounds off the doorstep of our motel. The capricious, frequently malevolent winds of Lake Nipissing could raise an awful lot of hell in that space.

So, for the first couple of springs, I just said "no," whenever the subject was raised. It simply seemed much too dangerous to me. With the kind of boats and motors our motel supplied, it would take the better part of an hour to cover that wide expanse of lake, and to get caught in a rising wind halfway across would mean very big trouble. Both times they grumbled a little, but went along with me in the end.

But the third year they were keener than ever to go, and my resistance was ripe for wearing down. That was a May that had decided to act like a July. When we arrived on the Friday evening there was a warm, benevolent softness in the air. A bright moon shone out of a cloudless sky, and when we strolled down onto the dock around midnight, in our shirt sleeves, the only less-than-perfect aspect was the premature presence of a host of determined mosquitoes.

Saturday dawned as if it had signed a personal-services contract with the President of the North Bay Chamber of Commerce. The sun shone down from an unmarred, delicately blue sky. The glass-smooth lake sparkled, and took obvious pleasure in reflecting it. The gentlest of breezes sighed through the still bare, but budding, branches of the trees.

To top it all off, the fishing off Sunset Point that morning was as good as any of us had ever experienced. It was merely reasonable to suppose that it would be even better out off the islands. And, if there was ever to be an ideal day on which to make the foray, that was surely it. I mean, what could possibly go wrong, what could conceivably happen of an untoward nature to a group of practical, reasonably intelligent men, on such a day?

And so I gave in, as I suppose I had known I would, sooner or later.

We set out around noon on that Saturday, the five of us — Frank, Oscar, Jack, Griff and me — in two boats: one a 16 ft., relatively new, aluminum job with a 10 h.p. outboard motor, the other an older wooden boat with a deck at the front. It, too, had a ten on the stern. Both boats looked small for that big lake, and I had one final twinge of anxiety as we were loading them up with our gear, but the decision to go had been made by then, and I knew I would have been hooted out of camp if I started up the argument again. I suggested that Frank, Oscar and Griff, the three real neophytes, take the slightly larger aluminum boat. Jack had had a little more experience, and he also had a kind of practical, native intelligence, so it seemed to make sense for he and I to take the cedar strip boat with the older, and possibly less-reliable motor. None of the others seemed to care much; anything was allright with them as long as we got on with the trip.

We made it out in about forty-five minutes, a laugher all the way. The sun was bright and hot in a cloudless sky. The two outboard motors purred reassuringly, as if they were ready to run forever. We ran side-by-side, the two bows cutting smoothly through the lead-flat, blue water. We took off our shirts, the better to luxuriate in the sun's warmth, and handed each other beers from among the ice cubes in the styrofoam coolers. There was a lot of good-natured, fishing trip repartee, much of it aimed at me.

"Sure as hell is rough out here, eh, Jack?"

"Bail for your life — we're goin' down by the stern."

"The stern's at the back, stupid."

"Anybody know 'Nearer my God to Thee'?"

I had no choice but to take it, my earlier trepidations a sore embarrassment on this tranquil, late spring day. The big lake was a phoney, all bluster, full of sound and fury, signifying not much. Hell, a ten-year-old kid could have paddled out there that morning in a wash tub.

It was something, too, to watch the islands rise up gradually out of the lake. There were five or six of them, the largest several acres in extent, plus a few smaller extrusions of rock. On one there was an angular piece of machinery, left from some abortive mining venture. A wide variety of water birds swam, and drifted, and flew around them. Isolated, unspoiled, there was a brooding, haunting quality about them that made me glad I had finally consented to make the trip.

If there was a sour note during the early afternoon, it was that the pickerel were not co-operating. We tried several likely-looking spots, but none of us managed so much as a nibble. Not that it mattered; it was enough just to be there. We went ashore for lunch on a clean, white, crescent-shaped beach, there to broil hamburgers and hot dogs, thrill to the primordial purity of the place, drink a few more beers, and ruminate expansively over why we had been so hesitant, so super-cautious, about undertaking the excursion earlier.

It was during that hiatus when I first noticed that the breeze was starting to freshen. The change was very subtle in the beginning, just enough to make the surface of the blue water shimmer with tiny wavelets. Ten minutes later the day was still benign in our sheltered cove, but beyond the point of the island small whitecaps were dancing from west to east. On the horizon clouds were forming up, like floats in the marshalling area of a parade.

I suggested that we might be wise to start back towards the mainland, but the others just sighed: old worry-wart at work again. Hadn't we got out there with no more danger than is involved in cleaning your teeth?

Another six hundred or so seconds ticked away. Frank, Oscar and the others were tossing a frisbee back and forth on the beach. They were relaxed, laughing. But, even on the lea side of our island, the water was becoming restless. And in the open lake, the rising wind was beginning to flick the foam off the crests of the building waves. In the west, the storm clouds continued to gather, and the advance guard was spreading across the sky. The lake and the wind were starting to flex their muscles in earnest. The North Bay shore was a long five or six miles, and maybe an eternity, away.

"Look," I said, supressing the nagging suspicion that we might already have waited too long, "either we go now, or we don't go at all. You guys want to spend the night out here?"

They still were inclined to think that I was exaggerating the seriousness of the situation.

"Allright," I told them, "stay, if you want to. You can have the big boat. Me — I'm leaving."

That did it.

"Don't get touchy," one of them said. "We came out together, we'll go back together."

We hurriedly loader our stuff into the boats, and shoved off. By then, though, I should really have been advocating that we stay where we were until the rising gale blew itself out — but that could be a couple of days. Our wives would be frantic if we failed to return to the city the next day, and the thought of the comfortable, dry cottage waiting for us back at Sunset Point was a lure that was hard to resist.

When we rounded the point of the island and started across the wide expanse of open lake, the two boats side-by-side, I thought at first that we were going to be allright. There was a pretty fair sea running, the waves probably a couple of feet high by then, but the wind was three-quarters behind us, so that we wouldn't have to take any swells broadside, and it seemed likely that, with sensible concentration on steering, and a reasonable amount of good luck, we would be safely home at the cottage, drinks in hand, pickerel fillets frying for supper, before the elements worked themselves up into a real rage.

That bit of wishful thinking survived, although growing progressively weaker, until we were somewhere around half-way back — about the point of no return, say, except that there never had been any prospect of going back to the islands — not against that wind. You could forget about swimming, too, with the water temperature about 40 degrees.

The sun had been gone for some time, replaced by low, racing, increasingly black clouds. The sparkling blue lake had become an angry, grey sea, the wind flicking the spume off the tops of the waves. The changing motion of the boat confirmed what my eyes had already registered — that the distance between crests was stretching out, and the depth of the troughs steadily increasing. The warmth was gone out of the day, too, and our thin sports shirts offered no protection from the chill wind.

The first time I admitted to myself that we were in really big trouble was when I glanced over and couldn't see the other boat. When it came back into sight a few seconds later, my feeling of relief was chillingly tempered by full awareness of the monstrous seas that were running on Lake Nipissing.

I managed to convey to Jack, six or seven feet in front of me, that he was to get down on the bottom of the boat. He did so, sitting with his back against the front seat, and his legs stretched out under the short bow deck. That would help to keep the weight low in the boat, and minimize the danger of going over. The real threat, however, was coming from the stern. The transom only provided a few inches of freeboard, and if the motor ever stopped, one of those big waves would come in over the stern and we would founder in seconds.

When I had time to think about it, I was still more worried about the three in the other boat than I was about Jack and I. None of them had had any experience with the kind of life-and-death challenge we were facing. Oscar, who had been accorded the task of handling their 10 h.p. outboard, was originally from Holland, and I remember thinking with sinking heart that Lake Nipissing in a storm was a far different thing from whatever he might have encountered on the canals of his native land. I tried to signal to Frank and Griff that they should get down on the bottom as Jack had done in our boat, but communication was impossible, even across the twenty-five or thirty yards which separated the two boats. By then, applying whatever experience, instincts, native intelligence, luck, and determination to survive Oscar and I could bring to the trial by ordeal, each of the two boats was on its own.

Before long, the exigencies of the situation precluded any further such philosophical thoughts. By then, every iota of physical skill, every unit of nervous energy, every ounce of mental concentration, had to be applied to handling that motor and that boat in such a way as to retain, moment by moment, whatever slender chance of survival Jack and I could still cling to. And, for the next twenty minutes or so, that chance fluctuated along a scale, the poles of which provided a range of from 'none at all' up to 'hardly any.'

To keep our boat from foundering, to safeguard the few precious inches which stood between survival and the sudden death which would certainly come if a single wave poured in over our motor-weighted transom, required an incredible and continuing combination of my sense of timing, the reliability and responsiveness of the motor under the most trying of circumstances . . . and the co-operation of the gods. As we wallowed at the base of each giant wave, I had to turn the steering column accelerator at precisely the right moment so that we might begin the ascent of — or the assault on — the next monstrous wave. To hesitate an instant too long meant that we would certainly, surely be swamped; to pour on the power a second too soon was to run the risk that the motor would die before we climbed up over the next crest. That sequence was repeated again and again and again, making outrageous, endlessly-repeated demands on both the motor and its operator. One lost all sense of time, and any other touchstone with normality. Later, Jack was to say that he had occasionally been able to hear my voice, above the raging storm, saying 'Holy Christ! Holy Christ!' over and over again. If so, it was more imprecation than blasphemy.

To this day I have no idea how Oscar, in charge of the other boat, coped with the situation. Perhaps he found the answers by reaching desperately, instinctively back through the mists of his genetic past, to a time when his predecessors were among the great explorers and seamen and navigators of all of recorded history. Perhaps it was blind luck, originating in the innocence of not fully realizing the dire desperation of the situation.

All I can remember is taking on those waves, fighting them one by one, never really thinking beyond the next, probably insurmountable, crest. And the shoreline of North Bay appearing to stay the same tantalizing, remote distance away. It must be like that for long distance swimmers, trying to cross Lake Ontario, say, or the English Channel.

And then somehow, incredibly, we were hurtling in towards the shore, the two boats no further apart than the width of a main highway. We could hear the surf crashing against *terra firma*. In the fleeting glimpses I could afford, I didn't recognize any features of the shoreline; it certainly wasn't within the familiar contours of the immediate Sunset Point sector. There were beaches and big homes, in the $100,000-plus price range, mostly California Redwood style. Astern, the giant waves continued to pile up, determined to swamp us before we could escape onto dry land.

Frank was trying to shout something across from the other boat. I couldn't hear, but somehow Jack picked it up and scurried back, crab-fashion, to relay the message to me.

Astonishingly, the others were concerned about a big sign on the beach towards which we were heading, which read: 'PRIVATE PROPERTY! KEEP OFF! TRESPASSERS WILL BE PROSE-CUTED!' Personally, I didn't care if the big house was owned and inhabited by Count Dracula.

I looked over at the other boat, shook my head vigorously, and pointed straight ahead.

"We're going in — right here, right now!" I shouted, the words snatched away by the wind.

Fortunately, Oscar appeared to agree with me, for he, too, continued on course.

The great rollers were piling up on the beach, reaching far back, almost to the foot of a fieldstone retaining wall. The two boats drove in, side by side, travelling at an alarming rate. At the last second I switched off the motor, and tilted it so that the propellor and shaft wouldn't catch on the bottom. In the other boat, Oscar followed suit.

The boat was carried up, up on the beach until I began to think the keel would never find the sand. When it did, we came to a jarring stop — the kind you make when you forget that the car you are driving has power brakes. We scrambled out into the ankle-deep foam and swirl-ing water, and pulled the boats as far as we could out of reach of the waves. We were all weak, emotionally and physically drained, thank-ful but incredulous that we had survived. Out there in that driving, carnivorous surf, still a half-mile from shore, I'm sure that each of us would have given long odds against ever seeing dry land again. I don't really know who had been more scared, the other four or I. On the one hand, it was a totally new experience for them, and they must have been utterly terrified by the angry vindictiveness of the storm, and the brutal power of the lake; on the other, I no doubt understood better than they that it had taken a miracle to get us all out of it alive.

A couple of minutes later a man came down from the big house, leaning forward into the wind as he walked. He was not Count Dracula, nor did he mention anything about prosecuting us. What he did do was take us inside and pour us generous shots of very good scotch. Later, he and a neighbour he recruited for the purpose drove us around to our cottage at Sunset Point. The boats would be driven back next day, or whenever the storm blew itself out.

We drank quite a bit of our own liquor, and about nine o'clock walked along Lakeshore Drive to a good Chinese restaurant we had discovered the previous spring. By then the wind had completely receded, and a bright moon was shining out of an almost cloudless sky. Over our meal, we talked about the storm and our near-thing deliverance. One thing we did *not* talk about, either then or at any future time, was a return trip out to the islands.

Strangely, though, that adventure is not usually what comes to mind first when something makes me think of the years we opened the pickerel season at North Bay. That distinction belongs to a completely different kind of an incident, and it dates from the very first May we journeyed to Sunset Point.

The year before, when Frank had gone there with his neighbor, the only real problem they had encountered was a distinct shortage of minnows. They would have caught twice as many fish, Frank reported to us, had the supply of minnows not run out by noon on the Saturday.

So, when we set out from Toronto on a Friday afternoon a year later, Frank had decreed that we would take our own supply along with us. We pointed out that the 225 mile drive was a long trip to ask fresh minnows to make, but he was not to be dissuaded. Consequently, we had six dozen minnows in two pails when we headed north out of the city. To keep those minnows alive we had to pull off the highway every hour or so and find a tap from which to change the water in the minnow buckets. Frankly, it was a hell of a nuisance.

Then, to add insult to injury, as we drew near to North Bay, it seemed that there was a sign every hundred yards or so along the highway, advertising fresh minnows for sale. Apparently the Ontario northland was experiencing its all-time record crop of bait fish that spring. When we finally got to our cottage, it was to find that the proprietor had a big tank on the dock in which there must have been a couple of thousand minnows — prime, lively specimens, selling for about half the price we had had to pay in Toronto.

Naturally, Frank got a lot of good natured kidding about the minnows — hauling coal to Newcastle, that sort of thing. Naturally, too, he assumed a defensive poise; having insisted that we transport the minnows all that distance, he was determined to tend to their well-being, so that they would be alive and well when we set forth in pursuit of the walleyes the following morning.

Consequently, the first thing he did when we checked into our cottage was to put the two pails in the sink, and turn on the tap so that a constant trickle of fresh water would run into the buckets.

We poured some drinks, and started up a poker game. A couple of hours later I went over to the sink to draw some water for the coffee pot. Out of curiosity, I opened the lids of the plastic pails.

The six dozen minnows were all floating on the surface, belly-up, quite dead, and a bright pink colour.

In his solicitude, Frank had turned on the hot water tap by mistake. Steam was rising, as from a lobster kettle, and the Toronto minnows were as thoroughly boiled as Frank himself became later that night.

12.
Catching Something to Catch
Them With

Frank's insistence upon transporting minnows from Toronto to
North Bay to open the pickerel season that spring may have been
carrying things too far, but most fishermen know that finding a supply of live bait can sometimes be a real problem, particularly when
you are operating in unfamiliar territory. What a surprisingly high
proportion of otherwise completely competent fishermen *don't* know,
however, is how to go about catching their own live bait, should they
find themselves in a situation where they can't buy what they need
from commercial bait dealers. I've heard of guys cutting short perfectly good fishing trips (or resorting to less productive artificial
lures), for instance, just because they ran out of minnows or whatever they were using, and had no idea how to forage for themselves —
even though the waters and woods around them were literally teeming with small fauna which would have fulfilled their needs perfectly
well.

Apart from making a fisherman self-sufficient, a knowledge of
how to collect his own live bait can save a cost-conscious angler a
significant amount of money.

Take the Lowest Common Denominator for all live bait enthusi-
asts, the no-nonsense, down-to-earth, unglamorous but always reliable, dew worm — or, as the Americans call them, 'night crawlers.'
Once upon a time you could buy them for a cent apiece, or a dollar a
hundred; nowadays they'll run you up to a buck-and-a-half a *dozen.*

Most are harvested by part-time, piece work employees working for entrepreneurs who operate under contracts with golf courses, parks, etc. The worms are held in refrigerated warehouses, sometimes for weeks at a time, then passed from wholesaler to distributor to dealer before they wind up on fishermen's hooks. By that time they are apt to be emaciated, emasculated, and as bored as a go-go dancer in an empty bar in a mining town on the night before pay-day.

Few fishermen seem to think of picking their own dew worms, probably because they don't know how easy it is to do. All you need by way of equipment is a flashlight and a can or other container to put the worms in. It's also advisable to have a spinal column free of potentially herniating discs, because the harvesting procedure requires that you spend a considerable time bent over from the waist, with your head a few inches above the ground. The final requirement is a recently watered or rained-on lawn, your own or a co-operative neighbour's.

For reasons known only to themselves, dew worms come out of their holes on nights when the grass is wet. All you have to do is walk slowly across the lawn, crouched ready for action, with flashlight and can in one hand, prepared to pounce upon an unsuspecting worm with the other. It is necessary to remember a few salient points. The night crawler will almost certainly have one end firmly anchored in its hole and, being very sensitive to movement, it can disappear faster than your change in the bar of a tourist trap hotel. The trick is to grab for the pivotal end to cut off the worm's amazingly quick retreat; go for the other, free extremity, and you're odds-on to come up with nothing but a couple of dewy blades of grass.

If treated properly, dew worms can be kept in good condition almost indefinitely. Put them in a tight wooden box in a mixture of loam and peat moss, placed in a shaded, reasonably cool location. Sprinkle a little water on the soil mixture from time to time, and add some rolled oats for nourishment. And keep the storage bin covered, unless you are willing to share your cache with the local bird population.

When I was a boy one of my tasks was to catch enough dew worms for the summer's fishing on the last couple of nights before the family deserted the city for the summer cottage. The worm box was located at one corner of the boathouse on the island. I suppose that, as the fruits of my labours, it would usually be stocked with five or six hundred night crawlers at the beginning of every summer. I don't know whether dew worms breed in captivity or not, but the supply always seemed inexhaustible.

Only once did I fall down in my worm-gathering responsibility. That happened on a night late one June after I had gone to see the original Frankenstein movie at the local Regent theatre. Around midnight I was crouched over my flashlight, reaping a good harvest of night crawlers on a well-watered neighborhood lawn. Beyond the tight circle of light under my nose, the night was black and limpid with inky shadows. A soft breeze stirred the leaves of the big trees overhead. And suddenly, with a realization that can still send a crawling sensation up and down my spine, I *knew* that monsters were as real as mustard plasters when you had a chest cold. Frankenstein was going to come lurching out of the night for me at any second. And so I took off the hell out of there, leaving the can of worms behind, and sprinted down the exact centre of the street for the sanctuary of our house. That one year we ran out of night crawlers by about the end of July.

As most fishermen know, crayfish are a fine, natural bass bait, and they can be found in almost any lake, river or stream. The soft shell variety are best, but the hard shells will produce fish, too, especially if you break off their pinchers close to the body. They like shallow water, where there are a lot of small, flat rocks on the bottom. In the daytime you'll have to turn over those rocks to locate them, and they are apt to be skittish and relatively hard to catch. At night, though, they come out of hiding and tend to be mesmerized by a flashlight beam, so that they can be gathered without too much trouble. When threatened, they will always scurry backwards — reverse being high gear in their automotive equipment. The trick, then, is to come on them from behind, moving your hand slowly through the water until near enough to make a quick lunge. The best way is to first pin them to the bottom, applying just enough pressure to prevent escape. Then turn your hand until you can grasp them between your thumb and index finger just behind the head, and lift them out of the water. Held in that way, it is impossible for a crayfish to reach you with his pinchers, a nip from which, while quite harmless, will usually cause you to release your hold, permitting your quarry to escape.

Frogs are another good bait and, like crayfish, can be found almost anywhere, almost any time. The little, green, leopard frogs, which become available about mid-summer, are probably the best, but the dull coloured swamp frog will do quite nicely in a pinch. Most anglers know that frogs rate high on the preferred food list for bass, but less well known is the fact that they are sometimes equally effective when presented to walleyes. Some hot summer evening, when the pickerel seem disinterested in minnows and night crawlers, switch to small, green frogs; you may be astonished at the result.

While frogs are simple enough to locate, no one, as far as I know, has devised an easy way of catching them. It still takes a fast hand, the willingness to slog around in ankle-deep mud, and a good deal of determination. Fortunately, because they are so plentiful, perseverance will usually put enough in your bait pail to satisfy your needs.

Personally, I don't use frogs for bait any more. There are two reasons for this. One August night a couple of years back I was catching some little, green leopards with the aid of a flashlight. This was up near Parry Sound, on the northeastern shore of Georgian Bay, close to the northern limit of the narrow band designated as 'rattlesnake country' in Ontario. Sensing a movement just beyond the circle of light from my flashlight, my right hand poised to pounce upon what I presumed to be a little frog. Then, at the last possible instant, I realized that there was something distinctly un-froglike about whatever was there in the shadows. Startled, I moved the flashlight enough to provide an impression of something mottled brown and black in colour, probably coiling or uncoiling, and unquestionably unpleasant. I'm not sure whether or not it was a Mississauga rattler. I didn't wait around to find out.

The other factor figuring in my decision not to use them any more is the disquieting manner frogs have of trying to push the barb of the hook out of their mouths with their front feet. Not only is there something much too human for comfort in this action, but it poignantly dramatizes their desire to be free and shows how much pain they are suffering. Maybe a hook hurts a minnow or a crayfish just as much, but at least the cruelty is less palpably apparent when you use them. Anyway, no more frogs for me.

Crickets make an excellent bass bait, and are easy to catch. So do the fat, white grubs which turn into June bugs later on. They can often be found in rotting tree stumps, or under old logs.

Many fishermen feel that the hellgrammite, the dark brown larva of the dobson fly, is the best live bait of all, but in my many years of fishing I've never encountered one in its wild state. And bait dealers are as jealously protective of their hellgrammite sources as trout fishermen are of their favourite streams. All the information elicited by my relentless and thick-skinned prying is that they are found in rivers rather than lakes. Beyond that, my only advice is to buy some whenever you run across a dealer with a supply on hand.

Some anglers swear by leeches, and I have no doubt they can be fish-producers, especially with smallmouth bass. Yet I will never get over thinking of them as blood-sucking parasites, and therefore too loathsome to consider. To each his own, of course, apart from the observation that all fishermen have a responsibility not to introduce leeches into previously uninfested waters where people like to swim without having to keep a container of salt at hand to sprinkle on the repulsive creatures in order to make them relinquish their suction-holds on human skin.

Minnows can often be caught, either by setting out a minnow trap overnight, or by employing a small dip-net in shallow water in the daytime. Both devices should be baited with a small handful of rolled oats. The trouble with a trap is that you won't know until the follow-ing morning whether or not you've succeeded in luring any minnows into captivity. Dip nets only work well when the surface of the water is calm, and the sun bright, so that you can see what is going on down below, and know when to haul upwards with all your strength. Both methods are worth a try, though, if you find yourself in some locale where the fish are ravenous and you have to replenish the minnow buckets through your own ingenuity and resourcefulness.

And, as mentioned earlier in the story about war-time trout fish-ing in Newfoundland, there is the humble grasshopper — the real *piece de resistance* of live bait. They work best when fished without a sinker, having then all the attraction of a perfectly presented dry fly, but with built-in action.

Dragon flies, or 'darning needles' as they are sometimes called, can be used for bass and trout, as can a variety of other insects. I know a man who once caught a good size largemouth on a Monarch butterfly.

So, given a modicum of initiative and inventiveness, there is never any reason to forsake bait fishing, even though the closest dealer may be a hundred miles back down the highway.

Even a strip of bacon rind will do in a pinch — if you're lucky enough to know of a store where you can still get bacon by the piece. And if you can afford to buy bacon of any kind at today's prices.

13.
Fit for a King

Everybody has seen a travel ad which claims that 'Getting There Is Half the Fun.' There is a parallel in fishing, about which it may be said that catching them is *only* half the fun, the proof of the rest being in the eating. Nothing beats a really fresh fish, just hauled out of lake, river or stream, and properly prepared by someone who knows his or her way around a skillet.

One of the finest meals I have ever eaten was prepared, not by a famous chef in an expensive big city restaurant, but by a Park Warden in the kitchen of his cabin beside a lonely, jackpine-rimmed, northern lake. Because he is a superbly independent, occasionally cantankerous man, who loathes publicity almost as much as he hates bureaucracy, we'll call him 'Will' and just say that the National Park he worked in was somewhere along the Great Shield between northern New Brunswick and the Rockies.

Actually, the meal was only one of many highlights of an extraordinary two days. Although related to 'Uncle Will' by marriage for several years, I had never met him until I walked up onto the verandah of his cabin and knocked at the screen door one early July evening. By then I had been on the road, looking for his place, for six or seven hours. During that time I had thumbed rides, including one on the back of a tractor, walked miles, forded streams, hitched a lift on a railroad jigger, repeatedly guessed at which fork to take at unmarked junctures along the ever-narrowing and increasingly little-used road. Along the way I had had some remarkable experiences. At one point a whole herd of huge, antlered animals had plunged noisily out of the bush and charged across the trail in front of me. Having never seen an elk in the wild before, and not knowing that there was a protected herd in the park, it was unnerving, to say the least, to be face to face with a couple of hundred of them at one time. A little later on I opened a gate in a sturdy wire fence, to discover a few minutes later that the black dots out across the flat grassland were bison, which I somehow outsprinted to a gate on the opposite side, slamming it closed in their faces.

By the time I saw the lights of the cabin I had been completely lost for at least two hours, and was disconsolately wondering how I could survive the voracious mosquitos through a long, uncomfortable night in the bush.

When Will answered the knock at his door, and I told him who I was, he took it as if it was the most natural thing in the world to have a nephew by marriage walk in unannounced out of the wilderness at nine o'clock on a Friday night.

I liked the man immensely from the first moment I saw him. Slightly built, not tall, clean shaven, skin leathered by countless hours spent outdoors in all kind of weather, Will likes to talk, is given to saying outrageous things in order to start an argument. He has no time for polite discussions. When I first met him, he would have been about fifty-five years old. He writes generally bad poetry of the Robert Service genre, raises rare tropical cacti and plants in the northern bush, reads voluminously, detests politicians, holds poseurs of every ilk in total contempt, makes everything from pen-holders to chairs from elk and deer antlers, and is constantly at war with his superiors — from the Park Superintendent to the Prime Minister. He also knows more about the bush, and everything that lives and grows in it, than any three people I ever met.

What he called his 'cabin' was considerably larger and infinitely more comfortable than that term would usually suggest. Constructed of stripped, carefully-fitted and varnished pine logs, he had built it himself some twenty years earlier. Consisting of spacious living room, well-equipped kitchen, and two bedrooms, it had pegged oak floors throughout. The ceiling was high and beamed. A floor-to-ceiling window ran all along the lake side of the living room. A wide fieldstone fireplace took up most of one wall, shelves of books the better part of another. Will had made most of the furniture, using a variety of native woods and his own designs, smoothing and polishing them to a fine satin finish. The cabin was as neat and clean as any home I have ever been in, yet there was a warm, non-antiseptic, lived-in feeling about the place that immediately put me at ease.

We talked for an hour or so, catching up on family news, touching on many other subjects. He told me, among other things, that the elk and bison I had seen were partially his responsibility. My account of seeing the herd of strange beasts cross in front of me amused him greatly.

"You were safe enough," he told me. "It could have been different in rutting season, though. They're capable of being pretty nasty customers when they put their mind to it."

"Actually I was a lot more concerned about the bison," I told him.

"Oh, they were just curious," he said. "They don't see too well, that's why they have to get up close. God knows how many millions of lives that must have cost them in the days of the buffalo hunters."

Suddenly he sat bolt upright in his chair.

"My Lord," he said, "I've got a brain the size of a thimbleberry!"

"How do you mean?" I asked, puzzled.

"Sitting here, yacking away like an old woman who just came out of the bush after a long winter. You must be starving!"

"Oh, no, not that bad," I told him.

"When did you eat last?"

"Well, I had a couple of sandwiches about noon," I said.

"Good God, why didn't you say something?"

"Oh, I figured we'd get around to it, sooner or later."

He snorted. "A man could be skin and bones by then. Matter of fact, I'm hungry, too. Had to pull a couple out of the lake. Damn fools managed to tip their canoe, and it as flat as a bowl of pea soup. Never did get around to making supper."

"Allright — my stomach *is* beginning to wonder if my throat is cut. Don't go to any trouble, though."

"Trouble, hell. What time is it, anyway?"

I said it was about eleven o'clock.

"What would you say to some chowder?"

"Sounds great."

"Pickerel should be off the dock right about now. Come on."

I followed him as he grabbed a rod from the corner of the room, and we went out onto the verandah and then down the twisting path

101

to his dock. He took one cast, very casually, with a red and white flatfish. There was a moon out by then and when the lure was about half-way in I saw the rod-tip jerk two or three times.

"Good," Will said, "too hungry to waste time."

A few seconds later a nice walleye, about two-and-a half or three pounds, was flopping around on the dock.

One cast, one fish.

"That should do it," Will said, starting back for the house with the pickerel hanging by the gills from his fingers.

"The way you hauled that out of there," I said as I walked beside him, "you'd think those fish were your own private stock."

He chuckled, "They are," he said, opening the screen door to the verandah.

Officially, the lake wasn't supposed to contain any game fish. He had stocked the lake himself, eight or ten years earlier, bringing the walleyes in from another lake twenty miles away, transporting them a few at a time in a big, old copper laundry tub. The transplants had taken to their new surroundings very well, spawning the first April, and increasing in numbers every summer after that.

"The fish experts down in Ottawa say this lake can't support pickerel," Will said, with unconcealed enjoyment. "I never did see any point in arguing with them."

"So nobody knows?" I asked.

"Just you, now. No reason to disturb those nice gentlemen in the capital. Anyway, if the word got out, I'd spend half my time filling out fishing licenses."

He cleaned the walleye, filleting it perfectly in about the time it would take you or I to turn the page of a newspaper. Then he chopped the clean, firm, white flesh into coarse chunks.

"Won't be long now," Will said.

He put the fish into a pot with some salted water and set it on the stove. While the water was coming to a boil, he chopped up an onion, a couple of potatoes, a carrot or two, and a green pepper. After about ten minutes he added these ingredients to the fish and water.

"Nothing like it to soothe an appetite fast," he commented. "Gets into all the cracks and corners."

"I guess not," I said. The aroma was beginning to make me feel weak.

Then, for a little while, he turned his attention to other things —

opening a couple of sealers he took down from a shelf, preparing vegetables, putting additional pots and pans on the stove, setting the table between other operations.

Soon he returned to the chowder, adding a cup of thick cream and several generous shakes of black pepper before setting the pot on the back of the stove to simmer. I found out later that he kept his own milk cow, which was the source of the cream and the sweet butter we enjoyed at supper, in a piece of pasture land not far from the cabin.

"Won't be long now," he said, over his shoulder.

"Umm, umm," was the only response I felt capable of making.

Not long after that, perhaps forty minutes after we had entered the kitchen, we sat down to supper.

No writer — not Shakespeare, nor Hugo, nor Aristotle, nor Steinbeck — could conjure up the words to do justice to the meal that followed. Uncle Will cracked a couple of bottles of home made wine — a white, concocted from lemon peels and potatoes, to go with the soup, and a red raspberry, as heady yet subtle as the finest Bordeaux, to accompany the rest of the meal.

The chowder — thick, steaming, rich, exuding delightful odours — was worthy of a sonnet, the pieces of fish and vegetables in the thick base thoroughly cooked, yet still firm. There followed a salad, built from crisp lettuce, radishes, green onions, slivers of carrot — all freshly picked from Will's garden behind the cabin.

The entree was elk steaks, cooked and preserved in thick gravy and onions the previous fall by a local woman who, for many years, had fulfilled the role of Will's 'housekeeper.' I never asked for a more precise definition of their relationship, but he and Irene were married some years later, and now she bosses him as nobody else could do.

With the elk steaks, tender and full-flavoured, we had tiny new potatoes, boiled just long enough to be no longer raw at the core, and kissed with a sprinkling of fresh mint; tender, young yellow beans; fried green tomatoes. There were thick slices of crusty, home baked bread to laden with the sweet butter. And a dish apiece of home preserved peach halfs in thick, sugary syrup. And chunks of locally-produced cheddar cheese.

I learned later that one of Will's regular tasks was to thin out the elk and bison herds each fall, eliminating the older animals who could no longer reasonably be expected to survive the rigours of a northern

Canadian winter. He never much liked this assignment, though recognizing the need for it. It took a skilled and patient chef, which Irene certainly was, to transform that sinewed, aged meat into the slow cooked, fork-tender steaks we ate that night.

Afterwards we went back into the living room. It grew chilly around midnight, and Will set some kindling and a couple of birch logs in the fireplace and got a good blaze going.

We drank a good many cups of coffee during the remainder of that night. Will made them in his own special way. Into the bottom of each cup he would pour an inch and a half or so of homebrew whiskey. In the matter of illegal stills, as in so many other things to do with the administration of the park, he made his own rules. Any local resident who made rotgut could expect to appear in court as soon as Will could track down his fly-by-night operation. But if he took proper pride in his work, ran a clean still, and gave his hootch time to age properly, he could look forward to a long tenure in the park — especially if he donated the occasional bottle to Will for personal testing.

To the booze in the bottom of the cup, Will added steaming hot coffee, slow brewed on the back of the stove. Then some of the thick cream, and a spoonful of wild honey, harvested from a secret source somewhere back in the bush.

The overall result was a nectar worthy, not merely of kings, but of the gods.

We sat up until somewhere around five in the morning, so that when I finally went to bed the first light of the new day was already tentatively probing across the lake beyond the cabin windows. We talked of mice and men and many other things that night — of poetry and politics and history and the mating habits of muskrats and whether or not there really are two distinct species of Northern Pike and the demise of organized religion and the likelihood that personal independence is the most sacred of all human values.

And, even if he hadn't rustled up the finest fish chowder to which man ever laid a spoon, Will would have become a very special friend of mine that July night.

He still is.

14.
The Dog That Was All Heart

Jim was what is usually called "a high ranking government official" in Ottawa, the kind of man who is well known to newspaper readers and television viewers, and is automatically invited to important cocktail parties in the environs of Capital Hill. For several summers he rented a delightful cottage in the Gatineau Hills, just across the Ottawa River in Quebec. Situated on a small, secluded lake, it provided a heaven-sent escape from the heat (climatic and political) of the city. You could drive there from the parking lot of the Parliament buildings in twenty-five or thirty minutes.

There were some memorable parties at that cottage, especially on Friday and Saturday nights. Jim and his wife, Marion, enjoyed entertaining convivial and interesting people, and there was always a crowd around on weekends — correspondents from the press gallery, parliamentary assistants, artists, writers, a scattering of MP's and Senators, and the occasional foreign diplomat and Cabinet minister. Once, at least, the Governor-General dropped by for a brief visit.

The atmosphere there was delightfully informal. When hungry, you helped yourself to food in the big, old kitchen — stew from a bathtub-sized pot on the stove, hamburgers from the barbecue, cold cuts and salad from the sixteen-foot harvest table. The bar, to which guests contributed their own bottles, was usually set up in the living room. There was often a card game in the evening — some kind of poker, nothing as serious as bridge. Occasionally someone would organize a midnight swim. On cool nights a cheerful log fire would crackle in the wide, fieldstone fireplace.

You could almost always rely on finding some stimulating, intelligent discussion in the course of an evening. You could *always* count on finding enough to drink.

One such gathering continued on until the slightly less than small hours of a Sunday morning. In the late stages the conversation had somehow swung around to trout fishing. There were only about a half-dozen hangers-on left by that time, and we were sitting out on the screened-in verandah. Nearby, Jim's dog, a big, floppy-eared, friendly mutt of incredibly indiscriminate lineage, was sleeping with one paw over his eyes. To preserve anonymity, let's call him 'Grundoon,' since nobody would have a dog with a name like that.

"If anybody's interested, we're practically sitting on the best trout stream I ever saw," Jim told us.

"Oh yeah?" I said, my ears pricking up, a habit they have acquired through years of being alert for hot fishing tips.

"It's a little hard to get into," Jim continued, "but there's one pool in there you just wouldn't believe."

It seemed that the stream was on a private estate, owned by a man *very* high up in Quebec politics, and patrolled by keen, not at all understanding, game wardens.

"I know how to beat them, though," Jim said.

Somebody suggested that getting caught poaching, especially by a VIP with different political persuasions, might not do his career any good, but Jim shrugged off the caution.

"The trick is to hit it early in the morning. Travel light, and get in and out fast."

So we organized a caper, the six of us, for the following morning which, by then, was only a couple of hours away. When Jim shook me, I thought at first that my head had fallen off, which, I concluded, on trying to sit up, might not have been a bad idea. Tousle-haired and bleary-eyed, my host was obviously not in very good shape either. But at least the two of us made it out of bed, which was more than could be said for our four erstwhile fellow conspirators, all of whom pulled the covers over their heads and said the hell with it.

We drank some coffee in the kitchen, then somehow found the

strength to dig some red worms in what had once been the vegetable garden.

It must have been a little after six in the morning when we went out to get into Jim's car. The sun had been up for a while by then, and you already knew that it was going to be a hot day. Although by no means thinking clearly, I was remotely disturbed by the absurdly minimal tackle we were taking with us. Apart from the can of worms, each of us had a small coil of nylon line, a few split-shot sinkers, and three or four light hooks secreted away in our pants pockets. That was all.

"You'll see," Jim reassured me.

Just as we were about to drive off, the dog, Grundoon, lumbered out of the cottage, yawning away the effects of his long sleep, wagging his tail, flopping his ears, and begging with his dark eyes to be allowed to accompany us.

"Damn dog has no brains," Jim said. "He's all heart, though."

I nodded agreement, again wondering if my head was going to fall off.

"Sit, Grundoon!" Jim commanded, sternly.

Man's best friend just wagged his tail harder.

"Sit, damn it!" Jim shouted.

Grundoon settled down on his haunches, his eyes larger than ever. For a moment I thought he might topple backwards, but he awkwardly attained a precarious balance.

"That's a good dog," Jim told him, putting the car in gear and nosing out of the driveway.

Twenty or so minutes later, we pulled off on the shoulder of a single-lane gravel road. To our right the ground fell away sharply into a narrow bush-flanked valley.

"This is it," Jim whispered conspiratorially. "Down there."

We got out of the car, and started to descend. The decline was extremely precipitous, a bit like coming down off the west slope of Mt. Everest, perhaps, except that Edmund Hillary and Tenzing Norkey didn't have to contend with mosquitoes, impenetrable willow thickets and prickly hawthorn bushes, the constant threat of game wardens, and monumental hangovers.

After a very long time — approximately, say, the duration of the reign of the Stuart kings — we finally emerged, scratched, panting, spaghetti-legged, heads throbbing and hearts pounding, on the margin of Jim's secret pool. Or, to be more exact, the one he occasionally shared with the lord of the manor. And I had to admit that, if ever I had looked upon a Shangri La for brook trout, I was seeing it then. Shadowed, mysterious, brooding, you just *knew* that it was a Mecca, which any self-respecting speckle would give anything to live in. I mean, there just *had* to be two and three-pounders lurking in those dark depths.

Jim produced a none-too-sharp pocket knife with which we managed to cut four or five foot willow gads. Moving very cautiously, so as not to spook the trout, we tied on the lengths of line we had secreted in our pants pockets. Then a split-shot sinker and a light hook. Finally a squirming, red earthworm. At last we crept forward, careful not to cast shadows on the water, prepared to present our offerings to those pampered, protected, illicit trout. The magic, hard-won moment, worth almost every agony of the morning-after descent, was at hand.

And, just at that most critical of instants, we were startled by a noise in the underbrush behind us. We swung around, our mouths open and our eyes wide. It was not just a little noise, of the kind which might be made, say, by a scampering chipmunk. Whatever was coming was barging through there like a rogue elephant. The thrashing and crashing around continued, while we waited, incredulously.

Finally, a shape, brown and black, and close to the ground, came hurtling out of the shadows. I caught an impression of floppy ears and large, anxious-to-please canine eyes.

Grundoon.

"Stay, Grundoon, stay!" Jim called to the dog, his voice somewhere between a firm command and a supplicatory whisper. Whatever the tone was meant to convey, it was just whistling beside the trout stream as far as Grundoon was concerned.

He bounded past us, looking for all the world like Pluto in the Disney cartoons, and leaped straight into the middle of the pool. Where he landed the water was quite deep and Grundoon had to dog paddle furiously to stay afloat.

"Drown, damn you," Jim said, half under his breath.

But Grundoon scrambled up onto the gravel of a riffle, between an old, half-underwater tree stump and a protruding slab of granite. If I were a big old brook trout, and could choose any one spot in the world as my home base, I would make a down payment on that pebbly shoal.

Grundoon struggled to his feet, bracing his sturdy, mongrel legs against the current. Then he twisted around to face us, his awkward body undulating violently to shake off the water.

"Oh, God," Jim said.

Grundoon regarded us triumphantly, waiting expectantly to be praised for what he had done. His tongue was lolling from his open mouth. His tail was wagging furiously, thudding against his scrawny flanks. He barked three or four times, just in case we'd missed his entrance. All heart, Grundoon.

By then, of course, every trout in the pool had taken off the hell out of there, probably out of the county. With that stupid dog standing there, drooling over the brilliance of his achievement, we would have had a better chance of catching fish in the lagoon in front of Toronto's new City Hall. In February. Or at the bottom of a bartender's ice bucket.

Grundoon barked some more; I think he wanted the game wardens to come and share in his triumph.

The two of us just stood there staring at him for quite a long time. Then Jim took his willow rod, broke it across his knee, and tossed the whole apparatus — line, hook, red worm and all — back into the underbrush. Mine followed a moment later.

"Well, Izaak," I said, "any suggestions?"

"Just one," he replied, "but it's a two-parter."

"Like what?"

"First, we try to make it back to the top of the hill."

"And, in that unlikely event?"

"We go back to the cottage and mix — oh, I'd say about a gallon and a half of Bloody Marys."

Which is what we did.

15.
Down the Muskoka River

Lou was a neighbor of mine for many years, the kind that you miss when his company finally transfers him to another branch a thousand miles away. We did a lot of fishing together during the decade or more that we lived on the same Toronto street. He was a big man, tall, stockily built, easy going, and, as he liked to put it "maturely bald." We shared a lot of interests — sports, good books, good food, the political scene, and an inclination to feel that crab grass has as much right to flourish as any other kind of vegetation. Lou liked to laugh. If you had a problem, and wanted to share it with him, it was his problem, too; if he had a case of beer, and you wanted to share it with him, it was your case of beer, too. In short, good company; an all-round hell of a guy.

Like all of us, though, he had a few shortcomings, a couple of which have a bearing on this story.

For one thing he was a compulsive over-planner. When it came to organizing a fishing trip, nothing could ever be casual, or impromptu, or left to sort itself out when the time came. I suppose you could say that he was a stickler for details — a sticky stickler. Each fishing foray was planned with the preciseness of a moonshot. No minutiae, however trivial, could be considered unimportant. Only with Lou could you wind up in a country general store, arguing about whether we should buy a can of sliced peaches, or a tin of halved peaches. Especially since neither of us liked peaches much anyway.

And he was certainly one of the laziest human beings I ever encountered. I don't think he would have jogged if he had been pursued by an All Star team of New Guinea headhunters. He had a reverance for physical comfort, and to him that meant having someone around to switch on his electric toothbrush. He was by no means physically inept or incapable; it was just that, to him, sweat and the exertion of manual strength were acknowledgements of a failure to exploit human intelligence. As far as Lou was concerned, if you couldn't enlist the aid of some mechanical device to get it done, or find someone else to do it for you, forget it.

A dozen years or so ago Lou somehow learned that a whole new, almost virginal, fishing territory was being opened up by the completion of Highway 103 from Waubashene to MacTier, along the southern portion of the eastern shore of Georgian Bay, in south-central Ontario. He was clearly excited about the prospect when he first broached the subject with me. We were drinking beer at the picnic table on his patio at the time. If we got up there before the inevitable land-office rush of tourists and cottagers, he pointed out excitedly, we would undoubtedly find walleye and bass fishing like we'd never seen before. The district was completely unfamiliar to me, but it sounded good, so I said to count me in.

We studied some maps Lou had picked up and decided that the best way would be to take a car-top boat up the new road to where it crossed the Muskoka River. From there we could work our way westward to Go Home Lake, and maybe continue on down towards Georgian Bay. I argued for a canoe, which would be a lot lighter and easier to handle, but Lou had made up his mind that a twelve-foot aluminum boat and his little 1½ h.p. outboard motor would be less strenuous, and, as previous experience had shown, there was no changing his mind in such matters.

We drove up from Toronto one Saturday morning early in July. The new highway was open beyond the Muskoka River, but it was still in a very rough state — only casually graded, with muddy and rutted sections, temporary bridges, and numerous detours. You're into the Great Shield up there, and the construction people were doing an awful lot of blasting. We had to stop repeatedly for demolition work, and to make way for trucks, graders, and great earth-movers, but we reached our destination well before noon without any significant misadventure.

The Muskoka was still a wilderness river then, beautiful, not wide, with the forest coming right down to the banks, placid for the most part but with intermittent stretches of shallow, impassable rapids.

While we were getting the boat into the water a yellow Department of Highways jeep came along and stopped. The man driving it was wearing a hard hat, and turned out to be one of the construction engineers.

"You fellas gonna do a little fishing?" he called out, amiably.

"Yeah, we thought we'd give it a try. You know much about the river?" Lou asked.

"Not a whole lot, except where we cross her right here. You should be okay, though. Just be careful steppin' over logs."

"How's that?" I called out, but he had put the jeep in gear and was pulling away in a cloud of dust and gravel.

"What do you suppose he meant?" Lou asked, looking after the jeep.

"Beats me," I told him. "Just warning us not to sprain an ankle on the portages, I guess. It's still pretty remote in there." I was by no means satisfied with that explanation, but there seemed to be no other logical reason for the remark.

So we shrugged and finished loading up the boat. As usual, Lou had brought enough stuff for an expedition to the headwaters of the Amazon, and the little aluminum twelve-footer was pretty low in the water when we pushed off. I can't remember for sure, but I probably made some scornful remark about his dinky 1½ h.p. motor — such as asking him why he hadn't brought along his wife's Mixmaster instead. Still it pushed the little boat along well enough, at least going downstream. It would be hard to imagine now, not much more than a decade later, when there are parking lots, and hydro lines, and nearby pizzerias and hamburg stands, but the Muskoka that day that Lou and I went down it could easily have been flowing into James Bay. We didn't see another boat. The wilderness came down to us on both sides of the river, unbroken and seemingly unviolable. Poplars, birches, pines, cedars. Bluejays screaming their warnings, and chipmunks scolding the bluejays. A small flock of Mergansers taking off as we came around a bend. A family of otters, playing on a point. A whitetail deer, turning away from the river, and leaping gracefully, with a sudden acceleration that no Grand Prix car could duplicate, over a patch of blueberry bushes and into the endless stillness of the bush.

We walked the boat through the first short stretch of fast water, guiding it along with bow and stern ropes. There was a short, awkward portage over uneven, boulder-strewn ground a little further along, then a longer one across the crest of a flat, worn granite ridge. The sun was high by then, and it was hot work lugging all of Lou's paraphernalia around the rapids.

We saw two snakes on that second portage. One slithered across the rock in front of us, the other crawled into a crevice beside a long fallen jackpine.

"What kind?" Lou asked.

"Not sure," I told him. In both cases I had had the impression of short, fairly thick bodies, and blotchy brown-and-black coloration. "Probably milk snakes." But they hadn't really looked like milk snakes, somehow.

"Can't be far to the lake now," he said.

"No."

We heard the sound of a waterfall over the chattering whine of Lou's little eggbeater when we were still a hundred yards or so up-river, and had plenty of time to nose in to the bank before the current really started to pick up.

There was that one final portage to make, but we didn't mind because of the sheer, unspoiled beauty of the place. The Muskoka River ended with a roar, not a whimper. Achieving their destiny, the waters cascaded down in a dancing, laughing fall of some twelve or fifteen feet, breaking into a zillion droplets on the rocks below. There was a deep, granite-encircled pool above the falls through which the current raced. Turning in the other direction, we looked out across the ragged, (then) unspoiled beauty of Go Home Lake. It was a sight to remember.

We had brought the boat and motor over, and were going back for the rods, tackle boxes, case of beer, lunch, movie camera, gasoline stove, portable radio, and God knows what else, when I noticed the sign nailed to a white cedar.

"What's that say?" Lou asked, joining me in front of it.

"My God!" I said, having begun to read.

The sign, posted by some government department, said that, in case of rattlesnake bite, the nearest anti-venom station was 14.7 miles away.

"Gotta be some kind of a gag," Lou put in, hopefully.

At that time there wasn't one Ontario resident in a thousand who realized that we *had* a rattlesnake population in the province. The Mississauga. Its habitat extends only along the southern and eastern shores of Georgian Bay, and nowhere ranges more than a few miles inland. It's a small pit viper, compared to, say, the Texas Diamondback or the Cottonmouth, and it is comparatively timid. Yet, if aroused to strike, its venom is, ounce-for-ounce, about as deadly as anything you'd ever want to come across.

The Mississauga rattlers had lived in innocent isolation for countless generations, glimpsed only occasionally by the odd prospector, trapper, explorer, or unusually intrepid fisherman. But the construction of the new highway had displaced them, stirred them up, made them edgy, bad-tempered and quick to strike.

Standing there, peering disbelievingly at the sign, we didn't know any of that. But I realized with sinking heart that I did know a couple of things. I knew what the construction engineer in the jeep had meant when he cautioned us to be careful about stepping over logs. And I knew why those two mottled shapes back at the long portage hadn't really looked like milk snakes.

I also had an unshakeable, intuitive conviction that the entrance to Go Home Lake might be a veritable Mecca — a Madison Square Gardens, a Metropolitan Opera House, a Nashville, Tenessee — for Mississauga rattlers.

By then Lou and I were looking all around us on the ground, our heads turning slowly from side to side, prickly sensations running up and down our spines. We finally told each other that we might as well give the lake a try; it would be silly to have come all that way and not even wet a line. But what we were really doing was putting off the time when we would have to make our way back over those portages.

"Snakes bother you?" Lou asked.

"Just the poisonous kind," I told him.

We stayed out on the lake until about five o'clock. I think we caught a few middling-size bass, but our hearts weren't in it. Even eating our lunch, a hundred yards from shore, we kept looking around uneasily; Lou had remembered reading somewhere that Mississaugas aren't averse to swimming.

114

We finally mustered enough courage to go in, only because we obviously couldn't stay out there on Six Mile Lake forever. Carrying the boat and other stuff back over the portage beside the waterfall, every root, every shadow looked like a snake. We didn't actually see one, though, or Lou and I would probably have run back to the car along the tree tops.

"I won't relax 'till I get back in the boat," Lou said. "Let's put her in right here."

"Hell, we're right on top of the falls," I told him.

"So what? Old Faithful here'll pull us through."

It seemed crazy to me. The water in the pool above the waterfall was swift and dark and you couldn't tell where hidden rocks might be lurking just below the surface. If that little egg-beater let us down, we'd be over the falls and heading for the rocks below before I'd have time to say 'I told you so.'

"I don't like it," I said. "No way do I like it."

"I don't like walking on rattlesnakes, either," Lou said. "Come on, let's go."

I knew that it was another argument I wasn't going to win. Once Lou's mind was made up, Aristotle, William Jennings Bryan and Attila the Hun, working together, couldn't change it. I scrambled over the case of beer and other impedimenta into the bow of the aluminum boat. Lou kept one foot on the rocky shore while he clamped on the motor, then gave the cord a yank. By some miracle it caught on the first pull, and he shoved off, then lifted his foot in over the transom.

The bow nosed out into the middle of the powerful current. He pushed the throttle all the way over, which is like saying that a caterpillar sprinted. Behind us I could hear the roar of the falls. The 1½ was doing its brave best, like The Little Engine That Could. The trouble was, it couldn't. The horrible realization dawned on me that we were just barely holding our own with the current, not progressing so much as an inch. We seemed to hang there for an infinity. At any moment I expected the tiny propellor to hit a rock and shear a pin. If that happened, we'd be gone to our glory before either of us had time to exhale. Lou was yelling something, maybe praying, but I couldn't catch the words.

Finally, ever so slowly, the boat swung over towards the far bank of the pool, coming up alongside it at last. I looked back at Lou. Still yelling, he was gesturing excitedly now with his free hand. I knew what he meant. My role in the pending tragedy was to grab onto the nearest available piece of *terra firma*.

I studied the rock wall beside me. Sheer, not a single handhold. But about seven feet up, just about as high as I could reach by standing up in the boat, there was a ledge. That would certainly provide the necessary purchase.

There was only one trouble; that rock collar was the finest piece of rattlesnake real estate I have ever seen. I just knew that, if I was a Mississauga, that ledge was surely where I would be hanging out. You bet.

And that left me in one terrible dilemma. If I reached up and grabbed the rocky prominence, I was odds-on to be greeted by a handful of rattlesnake fangs. And, if I didn't, we were a lead pipe cinch to re-enter Go Home Lake the hard way, over the falls.

I wish I could say I conquered my fear, but that would be wrong, because fear was going to win out, no matter what I did. I finally stood up, swallowed eight or nine times, closed my eyes, and groped my way up the sheer rock face with my left hand. Sweat was pouring down into my eyes.

At last my trembling fingers found the edge of the ledge. Nothing happened. No writhing, thick reptilian shape. No searing pain. No evil venom. I was almost disappointed; obviously the rattlesnakes of Go Home Lake and the Muskoka River didn't recognize a perfect habitat when it was right under their noses, or whatever they have up front beside fangs.

A few seconds later the egg-beater finally gained a foothold on the current. Slowly the little aluminum boat began to inch upstream.

Twenty minutes after that I had regained enough control over my shaking hands to open a couple of beers, and within the hour we were back at the car.

I've never been back there since. As far as I'm concerned, the Muskoka River can remain just a blue line on a map. And as for Go Home Lake, I'll stay at home, thank you very much.

I mean, with six months of snow and ice and no fishing to put up with every year, who needs rattlesnakes?

16.
Spawning Seasons

For me there is an unfailing fascination in the spawning habits of fish. Much has been written about the salmon in this regard — of the mysterious force that draws them back from the oceans to the head-waters of the streams in which they were born; of their determination in leaping over all barriers in their path; of the tragic process which sees them die in the very process of giving birth. But the intrigue extends to many other species as well.

Part of it, I suppose, is the association with the seasons; when the pickerel start to move up the rivers, you *know* at last that the blizzards and the grey days and the early twilights crowding in are things of the past, and that spring is really here. There is a vast reassurance as one gets older, in the expected rightness of it. That is why, one day towards the end of April each year, I always walk along the path beside Eel's Creek, through the woods still wet with the melting snows, where the trilliums are poking up through the flattened, brown leaves, to the rapids where the little river tumbles into the lake. Usually I do this with my cousin, Fred, who feels about these things as I do.

We stand there on the flat outcroppings of quartz, the planes and crevices of which are as much a part of both of us as the swirls of our fingerprints, and watch the walleyes fighting their way up against the swollen current of the runoff. Some, tails flailing frantically, make it on their first try; others, having struggled and been defeated, are swept back down, their white bellies flashing, to lie in the still, deep eddies until they regain enough strength to make another run at it.

We stay there, Fred and I, for a half-hour or so, letting the warmth soak through our open parkas, or shivering in the chill breeze of a cloud-roofed day that has not yet quite forgotten its January heritage. And then we go back to his place or mine and have a couple of drinks, which are always very special because of the shared, never-quite-to-be-assumed certainty that the loons will soon be returning, and the reflection of the summer moon will shimmer across the lake, and there could be a good crop of blueberries, and it will all look much the same as you nose your boat through the islands, and we will feel the hot July sun on our faces at least one more time.

When I think about fish spawning, a lot of other images are projected onto the memory screen of my mind. Sunfish, their tails patiently fanning little pockets in the sand of beaches, where they will deposit their eggs. A mother catfish, shepherding the hundreds of tiny black dots which are her progeny towards the security afforded by the gnarled, twisted, underwater roots of a long-drowned white pine, in the little backwater bay at the end of Rogers' Island. The big male bass, hitting Harry's dill pickle, as he would have hit the stump of Venus de Milo's arm, had it been thrust beneath the surface of that northwestern Ontario lake that June afternoon. Fat brook trout, lying as immobile as sticks of wood, disdaining the worms I drifted under their noses, in that deep pool on the Manvers stream one long-ago September morning.

Once, when I was a boy, a man who worked for the Department of Game & Fisheries let me go along with him as he set out to milk the sperm from spawning muskies for the government hatcheries. It was a prematurely hot afternoon late in May and, looking back, I suppose that he was glad to have a pair of young arms to work the oars of his skiff. This was on our lake in the Kawarthas. He sat in the stern, steering with a paddle, while I rowed from the forward seat. Between us, on the other thwart, there was a galvanized tin laundry tub, loosely covered by a sheet of canvas.

We went across the lake and worked our way into one of the shallow, stagnant, stump-studded bays that cut deep into the mainland. Soon there was barely enough water to float the skiff, and the keel kept grating on sunken logs. The water was like glass in there, and it was very still and silent, except for the cacophony of red-winged blackbirds in the marsh that rimmed the bay. Water bugs darted every which way in front of the bow. After a while I could row no longer, and poled us in further with one of the oars, the blade sinking deep into the mud and ooze on the bottom.

Then we saw the muskies. They were lying on all sides of us, perfectly still, their great backs barely beneath the surface. Some of them were huge — thirty, forty pounds, even more. They showed no fear of the skiff as we drifted amongst them.

The man from the Department of Game & Fisheries leaned over the side, and slid his hands carefully under the belly of a big 'lunge. Then he lifted it up, quite gently, carried it in across the gunwale, and held it over the wash tub, from which he had removed the canvas cover. The muskie betrayed no inclination to struggle, but just lay there in his hands, completely docile, as though in some kind of a trance. The man, who had done this many times before, moved one hand firmly along the belly, his fingers on one side and his thumb on the other. A spout of milky roe spurted down into the tub. He repeated this operation three or four times, until the 'lunge had been relieved of her eggs. Then he reached over the side once more and set her back in the water, letting her swim out of his hands. She stopped six or eight feet away to rest. A couple of minutes later her broad tail quivered and she started towards the open lake, stronger now, no longer lethargic, and was soon lost from view.

We must have milked thirty or forty muskies that afternoon, until there were a couple of inches of roe in the bottom of the tub, looking much like creamy tapioca pudding. I've never quite been able to reconcile the contrast between the placid mother fish I saw that afternoon and the way a big 'lunge runs and sulks and leaps clear of the water at the end of a casting line during the muskie season. The difference, approximately, between tigers and pussy cats.

The resoluteness of fish in spawning under unfamiliar and unfavourable circumstances can be a remarkable thing. The most amazing example I ever witnessed was at Clear Lake in Riding Mountain National Park, in northwestern Manitoba. Deep, clear and cold, this lake, which is large enough to get extremely rough in windy weather, is both fed and drained by underwater streams. Many years ago, lake trout were introduced into Clear Lake to provide game fishing for the hundreds of thousands of tourists who annually visit this beautiful, rugged yet handsomely tailored, wildlife preserve.

From the beginning, the lake trout fared very well there, growing deep-sided and heavy in the icy depths. In the absence of surface inlets and outlets, however, the fish were denied any natural retreats in which to spawn. There being the instinctive will, however, the big fish found a way, as I discovered early one September a few years ago.

At one end of the lake, well within the park proper, there was a 'wishing well', a circular pool perhaps twenty feet in diameter and two feet deep, joined to the lake by a narrow, very short neck of water. This scenic appendage was man-made, cement-bottomed and ringed around by a wall of manicured, flat stones. It was the kind of tourist attraction into which lovers and other people seem to feel compelled to toss pennies, nickels, dimes and quarters.

It would be impossible to imagine any place in which you would less expect to find huge lakers, grown to thick, sleek maturity on the bottom flats of a wilderness lake, except, perhaps, under the fountain in Rockefeller Centre in downtown Manhattan. And yet there they lay, twenty-five and thirty and more pounds. Their fins and tails and backs protruding up out of the shallow water, while dozens of late season tourists hovered above them and tossed pennies and tried to snap pictures to show the folks back home. I remember wondering how any of them would have liked it if a lake trout had forced its way into the maternity ward of his or her neighborhood hospital.

A few springs ago I was up in northern Ontario as one of the writers with a television production crew, filming an adventure series for family viewing. There were about fifty or sixty of us, and to-gether we swelled the population of the tiny town on the north shore of Georgian Bay to more than double its normal size. A production crew on location is a strange collection of people with diverse skills and talents — producer, director, cameramen, editors, electricians, make-up man, grips, actors, writers, continuity girl, prop people, drivers, accountants, sound engineer, typists and secretaries, animal trainers, and many others. And they represent as many personalities, temperaments, egos, sexual persuasions, loyalties, suspicions, inse-curities, fears and frailties. Thrown into close proximity for months on end, in strange surroundings far from home, working long hours under incredible pressure, human relationships are strained to the limit, and intrigues, political manoeuvrings, back-stabbings, and wounded sensitivities, are all endemic.

Still, our group got along better than most, and one incident which helped to knit it together happened very early in the game, only five or six days after the start of principal shooting. One of the editors, a grip, and I came out of the local hotel after dinner that Saturday night, wondering what we could find to do to put in the time until we could crawl into our beds and try for sleep. Apart from a couple of sleeping dogs, we had the hundred yards of the main street to ourselves. Everybody had seen the movies that were showing in Sudbury, fifty miles away. Nobody had much enthusiasm for bridge or poker. Dullsville.

Then, suddenly, from down by the river, there came a yell. "They're running! The smelts are running!"

Neither of my companions had the slightest idea what that meant, but we were all starving for any kind of excitement, and the other two scurried back inside the hotel to spread the word, whatever it was. A few minutes later a couple of dozen of us had converged on the river, and others were arriving — stumbling, tripping, skidding in the darkness — with every passing second. Included in our numbers were an English actress who had played bit roles in some very big box office successes, a fiery-tempered Irish assistant director, an aging character actor for whom the sun passed over the yard-arm about nine o'clock each morning, a couple of fairies, a property man who had rolled a jeep and was on crutches with one leg in a hip-to-ankle cast, and assorted big city dilettantes who, until very recently, had believed that the suburbs of Toronto lay in uncharted territory. Also included was 'Mr. Per Diem,' a small, ancient, black man of vaguely West Indian origin, who lived in the district, and had been hired to keep the books for the production. Also known as 'Poppa Doc' due to his happy but at the same time slightly evil and sinister smile, he was loved by one and all because he would cheerfully sign any claim for expenses placed before him. We were spending an awful lot of money in those early days — buying an airplane here, renting a whole tribe of Indians there — so that 'Mr. Per Diem' signed his name a lot of times each day. He laughed a lot, but nobody had ever heard him say anything. One day the executive in charge of all finances at the network back in Toronto phoned the Producer in a state of apoplectic indignation, complaining irately that the man hired to represent him on the production scene "would't speak English" to him! The Producer, who was accustomed to dealing with crises of the approximate magnitude of the Bay of Pigs several times each working day, calmly assured him that such was not the case. "No, no," he said, "it's not that he won't speak English; he *can't* speak English."

'Mr. Per Diem' and the rest of us peered out across the swollen, night-shrouded river. A young Indian was standing a few feet from shore, the water swirling around the knees of his waders, working a dip net. He lifted it up, raising the business end of the cedar pole above his head. Our eyes were becoming accustomed to the darkness, and there was a new moon. By its light we could see dozens of small, silvery fish, threshing, jumping, and wriggling in the drooping mesh of the net.

"What are they?" the English actress inquired across the few feet of water.

"Smelts. What do you think?" the young Indian replied, wading ashore with his catch.

"Can we catch some, too?"

"Sure."

"How?" the fiery Irish A.D. wanted to know.

"Get a basket, a garbage pail, anything," he told us, emptying the squirming smelts into a gunny sack. "They're runnin' good out there."

There was a sudden scattering, followed by a mad scramble around the nearby boathouses and along the main street to find anything that might be used to capture the little fishes — carton boxes, a wash tub, a length of chicken-wire ripped from around somebody's garden plot, a waiter's beer tray from the hotel, a hastily stripped-off shirt. Some primordial instinct urged us all on to harvest our share of the silvery bonanza.

Soon the whole gang of us were braced out in the shallow but fast water, crouched over, trying to scoop up smelts with whatever equipment we had managed to commandeer. It was like a gold rush, everybody scurrying feverishly to grab everything he or she could lay hands on. The English actress hauled up her skirt and used it to trap as many smelts as possible, storing her catch in her padded bosom so that she soon looked like an aging but turned-on sex symbol. The Irish assistant director worked like a man possessed, as he did in everything else; which is why he didn't last too long on the production. The potted character actor had to be rescued from a deep hole in the river bed, hauled out dramatically, but quite needlessly, by younger associates who had not yet learned that old drunks never drown. Through it all, 'Mr. Per Diem' ran back and forth along the river bank, smiling at everyone in the light of the new moon, willing to sign any piece of paper that might be placed before him.

It was a great evening.

The smelts, responding to whatever primordial urge, were swarming in countless numbers. There was the sense that they had been coming up that river each spring for countless eons of time, since a million years before the first image had ever been projected onto a picture tube; and that they would continue to swarm there, come May, long after the penultimate television series had been consigned to a dusty storage rack in some mouldering network headquarters. You could feel them teeming around your feet and legs. It would have been possible to take enough for several meals with your bare hands. They were there in countless thousands, maybe millions.

And then, suddenly, about ten o'clock, the run was over. One moment the water was alive with fish; the next there were none. Realizing this at last, we waded out onto the shore. Between us, we had harvested enough of the individually beautiful, glistening, six-to-eight-inch fish to put on a feed for a couple of hundred hungry longshoremen. Physically weary, we felt a little sheepish, yet strangely exhilarated, and somehow exalted.

"Let's go up to the hotel," somebody suggested. "Ray will cook them for us."

They all trooped away, excited by the camaraderie that had deepened in the couple of hours since dinnertime. I joined them after a while, and shared in a rare feast of tiny, golden brown fillets, washed down by vintage German white wine.

But for a little time after they had gone I sat on the bank of the river, bathed like the trees and rocks in the new moonlight, and thought about the myriad generations of smelts that had come to this particular stretch of water every spring to propogate and perpetuate their own kind. Since long before the mist-shrouded beginnings of the age of man.

And somehow that made the idiot-box series we were engaged in producing seem at once much less, and yet infinitely more, important than it had been before.

17.
Ice Fishing

Every winter, along about mid-February, I read about ice fishing in the outdoor columns of the newspapers, and get to thinking that I really should give it another try. Sitting in my warm living room, watching the drifting snow beyond the window, it seems like such a sensible way of breaking the long draught of the cold months. And some fresh caught whitefish, perch or herring would sure make a great meal. Sometimes I even jot down the name and telephone number of some fish hut operator up on Lake Simcoe, which is only an easy hour's drive north of Toronto.

But I don't really think I'll go again. I did try it a few times some years back, but to tell the truth it just isn't my cup of tea. Oh, I know that a lot of people get a great deal of enjoyment out of it, and I envy them. But for me fishing huts, which are always too hot if you keep the door shut and too cold if you prop it open, are claustrophobic places. You sit there in a kind of perpetual gloom, with the walls closing in around you, and you can't see out through the small, steamed-up windows. There's the dampness, and the smoke gets in your eyes, and the odour of heating oil fouls the air. It just doesn't seem like fishing, somehow.

Anyway, the last time I went I got the hell scared out of me. There is always something terribly unnatural, though exciting enough in its way, about heading out of the city on a fishing trip while winter still grips the land. If you're like me, you associate fishing with open car windows, and roadside picnic tables, and happy families heading for the cottage, and boat trailers and campers, and lush green countryside. With a time when the living is easy. But, heading up Highway 48 that morning, the trees were still stark and bare, the cornfields and pastures were deep in snow, many of the fences were buried, and there was the sense of a short period of daylight, which is the curse of all people who live in the northern latitudes; the days were growing longer, sure, but the telecasts of the NHL games still started well after darkness had closed in around bars and rec rooms. Rationalize as one might, it was still very much winter.

Around ten-thirty I drove in along the snow-rutted road to the establishment of the proprietor of the ice fishing huts. His wife gave me a cup of coffee, and offered bacon and eggs, which I declined. We talked, the three of us, at the counter of the tiny restaurant. Business had been slow, but the fish had finally started to bite during the last week or so. His huts were clustered about four miles offshore. He would take me out there and, as part of the basic service, pick me up just before nightfall. Since it was a mid-week morning, I was his only customer. We said goodbye to his wife, then walked the few feet out to his somewhat antiquated bombardier, a half-track which long pre-dated snowmobiles. It was a little claustrophobic, and there was a strong smell of gasoline, which didn't discourage my host from re-peatedly relighting the stub of his cigar. When we started out the sun was bright, sparkling off the ice and drifts so that it would blind you if you looked into it for any length of time, and there wasn't even the suggestion of a wind. Very still and tree-snapping cold. On the run out we talked as best we could over the noise of the slightly-wheezing old motor; the ice, he said, had been slow in forming that winter, and even at that late date there were still dangerous faults and slushy holes to threaten anybody who didn't really know the lake.

We reached the cluster of huts about eleven o'clock.

"All empty," the proprietor told me. "A couple of guys had re-served the one next to yours, but they cancelled out last night. Wife sick, or something."

Other huts dotted the horizon of the frozen lake, but none closer than a quarter of a mile as best I could judge in that flat expanse.

He helped me carry my gear into the hut he had designated as mine, then took his leave.

"Be back just before dark, long about five-thirty or so," he said. "Good luck, and enjoy yourself."

I stood at the door and watched him go, the old bomardier gradually growing smaller as he headed back towards shore, and I felt very much alone in the empty, silent, frozen desert of the lake. Finally, when I could see him no more, I turned and went inside.

The hut was well built and comfortable by ice fishing standards, with a propane heater that was easier to regulate than most. I made a pot of coffee on the gas stove, then settled down for a long, leisurely afternoon. From what the owner had said, I was optimistic that I might run into some respectable fishing action; apparently the herring had been co-operating all season long, and the lake trout had started to hit with some consistency over the past week or so. He had chummed the holes with salted minnows the previous evening, and there had been no one out there since.

I tried a jig for the first hour or so, without success, then switched to small, live minnows, and settled back to wait for the tip-up to tell me that something was happening down near the bottom beneath the ice. Only writing is as lonely as ice fishing.

A couple of hours later I poured myself a rum from the pint I had brought with me, and set about making lunch, which involved nothing more complicated than opening a can of beef stew and unwrapping my sandwiches. I knew from past experience that you tend to get pretty hungry sitting in an ice hut, but I would be back on the mainland in time to enjoy a good steak for dinner at some highway restaurant on the way home.

I got a couple of light nibbles early in the afternoon, but nothing that could be considered a real bite, and by three o'clock I was beginning to consider the likelihood of being skunked. Then the flag on the tip-up began to jiggle in earnest, and moments later I hauled my first fish of the day up through the hole. It was a whitefish, as I had suspected from the gentle way it mouthed the bait — about two pounds, nice eating size. Two others, virtual twins to the first, followed in rapid succession, then the brief flurry was over.

When I took the fish to the door to lay them on the snow outside, I noticed for the first time that the weather was undergoing a pronounced change. The sun was gone, low, dark clouds had spread across the sky, and the wind was rising. As I closed the door, my first feeling was one of surprise; the morning weather forecast had promised clear skies through to the following afternoon. As I learned later, a storm front had moved in from the southwest much more rapidly than anticipated. At that time there was no sense of concern; in less than an hour I expected to be on my way back to the mainland and, a little later, a very dry martini and a medium-rare sirloin — with lots of sour cream on the baked potato. Sure, the wind was whistling beyond the flimsy ice hut walls, and the first flakes of snow were swirling past the small window; but the blizzard, if it did develop, was something I would read about in the next morning's paper in my living room back home.

By the time four o'clock came, however, the situation had deteriorated drastically, and we had what a South Carolina friend of mine would describe as "a whole 'nother batch of home-brew." In the space of an hour, the wind had risen to gale force. The teeming snow, driven almost horizontally, limited visibility to a few feet. A white-out.

For a time I clung to the belief that the hut operator would find his way out, turning up in his wheezing half-track to rescue me. After all, he knew each square foot of the lake, understood its every mood and whim, could anticipate its tricks. I didn't want to admit of the possibility that he, too, might have been lulled into a sense of false security by the perfidious weather forecasts.

An hour later I had to accept the fact that he had not merely been delayed. Not even a penguin could find his way through that storm, and he would not be coming until the blizzard blew itself out. Still, that could only be an hour or so, two or three at the most, and then I would see the headlight of the half-track probing across the ice and snow. In the meantime, I was sheltered, warm, safe, and needed only to fight off any irrational, needless tendency to panic.

By about eight o'clock I was willing to concede that my chances of eating a medium-rare sirloin that evening were about as remote as the probability of Tristan da Cunha's winning the world's hockey championship. But there was no reason to go hungry, and I set about making an inventory of the resources at hand. There were, of course, the three whitefish, frozen and buried in snow, just beyond the fish hut door. There was lots of coffee. A check of the makeshift cupboards revealed that previous incumbents had left a quarter of a pound of margarine, some powdered eggs, a plastic bag containing bread crumbs, and a package of freeze — dried green beans.

I pumped up and lit the gasoline lamp that was hanging from the roof, and set about making dinner in the reassuring light. It didn't take long to prepare the whitefish for the frying pan. I made a palatable batter from the powdered eggs and some tinned milk I had brought, dipped the fillets in it, then rolled them around in some of the bread crumbs. All the beans required was to be heated up in some water. I poured a pre-dinner rum, then set the pieces of fish to sizzling in the margarine.

Under the circumstances it turned out to be a pretty good meal, and I ate it with relish at the little, fold-down table. A little later, over after-dinner coffee, I listened to the blizzard howling outside and luxuriated in a sense of comfortable well-being. At that time I still thought that I would be sleeping between my own sheets before the night had passed.

By midnight, however, I knew that it was not to be. Beyond the fragile walls of the hut, the storm raged on with uncompromising fury, as if it might never slacken. Around one o'clock in the morning the gasoline lamp sputtered and died, its fuel supply exhausted. About then, sitting in the sudden, terrifying darkness, hearing the wind howling outside, I came face to face with the fact that Jimmy the Greek would probably offer no better than even money on my chances for survival. There certainly was no way out; Frobisher wouldn't have lasted a hundred yards in the face of that bitter sou'wester. Apart from the fact that you couldn't see your hand in front of your face, the temperature was probably edging down towards zero, maybe thirty or forty below if you took the wind chill factor into account. Very simply, my prospects of witnessing the next morning's dawn depended upon how much propane gas remained in the canister which fed the heater. If that ran out before morning, I would die, as certainly as female salmon must die as they return up their mother rivers and streams to spawn. There would be a gauge, I supposed, to indicate the burning time left, but I stubbornly fought off the natural tendency to look for it; what possible good could it do me to know?

The cutlery was kept in a drawer of the small table and, groping around in there to find a spoon with which to stir my coffee, my fingers discovered a flashlight. The batteries were pretty weak, but there was enough power left in them to throw a circle of pale, yellowish light. On balance, it might have been better if I hadn't found it because it permitted me to look at my watch every now and again. The night passed with incredible slowness. I would check the time, wait for an hour to pass, look again — and find out that it was only ten minutes later.

With nothing to occupy my mind, I worried about real dangers and invented imaginary ones, including the possibility of drifting away on an ice cake — which, of course, was impossible, since the lake had been frozen solid for two months. The worst thing was the cracking of the ice. I suppose it was tightening up with the drop in temperature. When a fault developed, you could hear it running right across the lake, sometimes seeming to start miles away, growing louder as it came closer, closer. It was an almost indescribable sound — a sharp yet prolonged boom; something, I imagine, like the report a jet plane makes when it breaks through the sound barrier. It was easy to imagine a crack opening up right under the hut, wide enough, perhaps, to drop it and me into the icy depths below. There were other loud noises, too, like something crashing, which I couldn't identify at that time. And all the while the howling of the wind. Alone in the tiny, frighteningly finite confines of the hut, I felt cut off from the world; what was going on out there? Who was worried about me? It was like being in jail.

My eyes were heavy-lidded, but there was no thought of trying to get any sleep; the only place to lie down would have been on the cold, hard floor, and I felt I should stay awake in case of an emergency — although God knew what I would do about it, should one arise. The wind occasionally probed through cracks and crannies, leaving miniature snow drifts here and there, but it was warm enough in the hut — would be as long as the propane for the heater held out.

In what seemed at the time to be a matter of considerable importance, I had decided to save the last of the rum to be drunk at five o'clock in the morning. That, I reasoned, would probably be about the low point in the long night; yet, at the same time, having reached it, I would only have a couple of hours left to go until first light. Alone in the darkness, with the ice booming every few minutes, and unwelcome thoughts of an icy death doggedly pushing their way into my mind, it was vital to have a landmark to shoot for and to retain the prospect of a small reward. I must have looked at my watch a dozen times between three and four o'clock.

When the magic hour finally arrived, it touched off a whole series of events, all of them upbeat, foreshortening the remaining time.

Savoured slowly, the warmth of it welcome in my throat and stomach, the rum itself was much appreciated, restoring confidence and providing a sorely-needed touchstone with normality. Then, just as I was draining the last of it, something told me that the tip-up was signalling action down below. At first I thought that I was imagining things, my mind playing tricks after the long night. Although I'd kept the hole free of ice, largely to give myself something to do, it had been many hours since I'd last given any serious thought to fishing, and the pre-blizzard minnow must have been long since dead. But the flashlight beam confirmed my intuition; the tip-up was dancing around like a 1944 jitterbug.

I felt the weight of the fish as soon as I picked up the stubby rod, knew it was considerably larger than the three I'd caught twelve hours earlier. Five minutes later I managed to haul it up through the hole onto the floor of the hut — a brightly-spotted, silver-sided lake trout of about eight pounds. Almost as soon as the rig was down again, baited with a fresh minnow, I had another fish on. Considerably larger than the first, it broke free about half-way up, but I pulled out a six-pounder a few minutes later. It was a strange way to fish, groping and stumbling around in the dark, but I enjoyed the spurt of excitement. I fished for a while after that, but the flurry was over and there were no more bites.

When I opened the door to put the fish outside, I realized that the blizzard was about over. The snow had almost stopped and the wind, though still gusting with some of its earlier virility, was betraying a willingness to lie back in bed and tell patriarchal tales of what it had once been.

I closed the door and made a pot of coffee, there being just enough tinned milk left to lighten the second cup. By then the first pale greyness of the new day was leaching away the darkness beyond the window.

I heard the half-track when it was about half-way out from the mainland, its roar coming clearly across the sudden stillness. When he got there, the proprietor was extremely solicitous about my well-being, and eager to have my endorsement that he could not be blamed in view of the misleading weather forecast of the previous day.

I assured him that my survival had been no big deal for a veteran, resourceful outdoorsman, not bothering to add that I hadn't exactly felt that way about three o'clock in the morning.

130

We walked through the drifts to the half-track, the tails of the two good trout trailing over the snow and ice on either side of me.

"I figure you had enough propane for maybe another three or four hours," he told me.

"I never doubted it," I said.

"Sure glad she didn't go over like them two," he added, nodding over to our right.

I looked in that direction, and there were two huts lying on their sides, one with its roof half off, the other buckled so that pots, pans, chairs and other debris had spilled out over the ice. I tried to imagine what it would have been like in *my* hut, if that had happened to it. What if the two guys with reservations *hadn't* cancelled?

"Lucky thing the stoves weren't lit," the proprietor said. "Those huts'd sure have gone up like kindling."

All of which goes to explain why I don't get around to calling those phone numbers of the ice hut operators that I jot down from time to time.

It's not, of course, that I've been frightened off ; just that my wife would worry if I went again.

18.
Be Good to Your Guide

To many of us — desk-bound executives, for example, and factory workers, lock-stepping their days away on assembly lines — being a fishing guide sounds like one of the world's best occupations. How many ways are there of getting paid to do something you would gladly do for nothing? As King Clancy asked, when signing his first N.H.L. contract, back in the twenties: "You mean they're gonna give me money to play hockey?!"

And, although not recommended as a step towards becoming a financial tycoon, it *is* a pretty good job most of the time. The majority of clients are willing to treat you as a competent professional, accord you reasonable respect, let you keep whatever dignity you may consider important, and take their fishing luck as it comes. Unfortunately, as every prostitute comes to know, once you hang out your shingle, you more or less have to take on all comers; and that can mean working under some pretty unpleasant individuals.

I spent a couple of summers in the trade, long enough to learn most of the ropes, and I pass along this tip, free of charge: if you want to get your money's worth, be good to your guide. Believe me, he can make your fishing trip, or break it. Think of it this way: sitting in a dentist's chair, waiting for the freezing to take so that you can have root canal work done, is no time to insult good old Dr. Dortmunder, right?

Be pleasant with your guide, and you can be reasonably sure that he'll do everything in his power to get you fish — especially if you've laid a few extra bucks on him at the start. He undoubtedly has a few secret holes, sure-fire producers, which he saves to turn to as a last resort when all else fails, and these will be available to you *if* he's come to the conclusion that you're a reasonably decent human being. One guide I knew used to look upon a government fish sanctuary as a private preserve to be shared with his most favoured clients. A big, weedy bay, closed off from the main lake by a heavy, steel-mesh net, and clearly posted by the Department of Game & Fisheries, it had more big 'lunge than Maple Leaf Gardens has hockey fans on a night when *Les Canadiens* are in Toronto. If the fishing had gone poorly during the week, Pete would slip in there just about dusk on the final evening — when the light had faded sufficiently to mask the official signs. He would explain the need to tilt the outboard motor, as the boat glided over the net, by saying that there were a lot of treacherous shoals at the entrance to the bay. Once inside, hooking a good fish was about as difficult as rolling over in bed.

And, later on that evening, back at the Landing, the client would shake his head and say: "Well, you came through again. Left it until the eleventh hour, though." And Pete would just smile innocently, the way guides often do when they're giving you the business.

On the other hand, the man who is surly with his guide, plays the big shot, neglects to share his beer, or is otherwise unpleasant, is apt to spend most of his week casting or trolling in waters containing about as many fish as an Olympic pool. The places he is taken to will *look* as if they should be productive, but they will all be ghost towns as far as the bass, walleyes and muskies are concerned.

With such an undesirable client, the guide is apt to shake his head every so often and mutter something about how unfortunate it is that the muskies are losing their teeth just at that time.

"Should have been here last week," he'll say. "Really hitting, the 'lunge were then. Or if you could come back in a few days. But right now their mouths are too sore, you see."

There must be hundreds of fishermen scattered around the United States who still believe that their fishing treks into the wilds of Ontario were spoiled because the big fish shed their incisors at a particular time each summer. There would not, however, be any consensus as to when that remarkable annual event occurs, some placing it in early July, others insisting on mid-summer, still others swearing by the end of August. The truth is, of course, that muskies are about as likely to lose their teeth as weightlifters are apt to lose their appetites.

As a general rule, though, a guide would rather have to put up with a boorish client than be forced to suffer an incompetent one. The former can make a week seem much longer than seven days, but the latter are sometimes downright dangerous. One summer many years ago a friend of mine named Sonny was inflicted with a greenhorn from Cleveland who insisted on casting sidearm. This meant that Sonny, in the stern of the boat, was constantly forced to duck as the big plug went whistling close above his head. Three times the old fedora he wore was snatched from Sonny's head, the hooks narrowly missing his scalp on each occasion. Three times Sonny asked his hopeless client to be more careful, pointing out that his fifteen dollars a day didn't include any allowance for danger pay. The fourth time it happened, Sonny didn't say a word; he just walked up to the front of the boat, snatched the fishing rod from his client's hands, broke it across his knee, and threw the pieces into the lake. Then he headed the boat for home as fast as it would go.

One of life's more pleasant experiences is to sit in the shade of a tree on a sunny summer day, drinking a cold beer, perhaps, and watch as your guide goes about the business of preparing a shore dinner. Many guides make their own wooden carrying cases, taking considerable pride in the neat, efficient way that pots, pans, cups, dishes, cutlery and the other essential equipment is stored inside.

First, the guide builds a circular fireplace of flat stones. Then he gathers the wood, some light stuff for kindling, a few driftwood pine roots for real heat and staying power. While the fire gets going, he will be busy cleaning the fish, opening cans, preparing vegetables, slicing bacon from a slab, setting out the dishes and knives and forks, putting water on to boil for the tea or coffee.

A good shore-dinner chef, and there are some real artists among the guides, doesn't waste a motion, and never seems harassed, as he flits from one chore to the next, starting things at different times so that the whole feast will come together at the climactic moment.

Ah, the sights and sounds and smells of a shore dinner! The flames leaping and crackling under the pots and pans on the metal grill. Steam rising. Bacon sizzling. The delicious aroma of onions frying in the open air. Walleye filets taking on a deep, golden-brown crust in the hot fat of a frying pan. Sliced potatoes, bubbling and frothing towards crisp perfection, in another. Maybe a pot of beans, cooked the previous day and thick with chunks of salt pork, warming to one side of the grill. Freshly sliced bread; with luck, homemade. A whole pound of butter. Hunks of cheddar cheese. Perhaps an apple or blueberry pie, baked with lard and lots of sugar, and a disdainful ignorance of calorie charts, by the guide's wife.

One of the finest dishes I have ever eaten was a shore dinner concoction originated by Sonny. The base was canned pork and beans; approximately one tin per hungry participant. To that, he would add fried onions, crisp bits of bacon, fresh or tinned tomatoes, a touch of garlic, a generous dash of Worcestershire sauce, maybe some ground meat, or rice, or whatever else might be at hand, and lots of catsup. And chili peppers.

A couple of helpings of Sonny's special Stoney Lake dinner and you were guaranteed not to get a cold through February of the following winter — maybe not for the rest of your life.

Given a boorish client, though, Sonny could become the most incompetent shore-dinner cook ever to hold a guide's license. It was a mysterious, Indian thing; he would just suddenly be unable to do anything right. The home fried potatoes would burn to cinders. The tea would taste like swamp water (which it was likely to be). The fillets, in the unlikely event that the client caught any fish, would be undercooked. The canned beans would be barely warm.

"Son of a gun," Sonny would say at such times, "I guess I forgot to bring the salt."

He had a weird sense of humour which helped him to secretly preserve his dignity when it came to coping with bad clients.

One man from Ohio, a doctor as I recall, got charred canned meat, almost raw fried potatoes, and cold beans for ten or eleven straight days.

Another time, for a particularly unpleasant couple from West Virginia, he served a stew that he had prepared in advance and re-heated over the campfire.

"Something special," he told the man and woman. "You won't get this very often." Which was true enough.

"It's delicious," the woman said, trying a forkful.

"It certainly is," agreed the man. "What's the meat?"

"Guess," Sonny suggested.

The man, a highly successful pharmacist, speared a chunk from his plate and held it up for closer examination.

"Rabbit?" he suggested, tentatively.

Sonny shook his head in wonderment.

"I should have known I couldn't fool you," he said.

But then, I don't suppose I'd recognize skunk meat if I saw it in a stew, either.

19.
No Place for a Muskie Fisherman

A couple of springs ago I drove down to visit my twin sons, who were attending the University of Texas on track scholarships. It was mid-March, windy and snowing, when I left Toronto, and the joy of driving into spring — the grass greener with every hundred miles, buds breaking out into leaf, forsythia yellowing the roadside in Cincinatti, flowers in full bloom in Lexington — was something every northerner should experience at least once.

On the evening of the third day I checked into a motel in a small city in southern Arkansas. In the process of registering, I got talking to the owner, and we weren't long in discovering that we both liked to fish. I told a few lies about the size of the muskies in Ontario — just slightly smaller than bluefin tuna — and he laid a couple of tall tales on me about his own experiences. I think he had been into the redeye pretty good that afternoon and early evening, but that, of course, is never anything to hold against a man — particularly one who likes to wet a line on occasion.

"Don't reckon y'all are familiar with hoggin' up there," he opined. (It might have been 'hawgin;" I don't know, because I never did see it "writ out".)

"Can't say as we are," I told him.

"Jest 'bout the best sure-as-hell fun you're likely to come across," he added, producing the bottle of sour mash and plopping it down, neighborly-like, in front of me on the counter.

"I don't doubt it," I said, pouring myself a generous slug of the paint remover.

"Y'all'd like to try it, me and Luke was figurin' to go out come moanin,'" he said. "Count it a pleasure to have you along — less'n you got reason to put a lot o' miles behind you, real quick."

I wasn't due in Austin until late the next day, and could afford a few hours for a new experience.

"Reckon I'd like that," I replied. Honest. The bourbon was causing second degree burns to my throat, and I doubted that a doctor could build up much of a practice from tonsillectomies in that part of the country.

I asked him to tell me about it, this hoggin,' or hawgin'.

"Do better than that," he said. "Got some movies the little lady took one time last year. Get settled, then come on back down."

"I'd like that," I told him.

"Clara, come on out here and take care o' this place a spell, y'hear?" he shouted, as I was leaving to go and find my room.

When I returned, he had the Super 8 movie projector set up in the living room off the motel office. The bottle of bourbon and our glasses stood nearby. There was one of those black velvet paintings on the wall, flanked by an embroidered 'Jesus Saves,' done in red, white and blue, on one side, and a pair of china ducks on the other.

My host switched off the lights and started the projector. Shot by unsteady hands and featuring a lot of rapid pans, Clara's film was never going to gain an Academy Award nomination for best short subject, but it proved adequate to give me a good idea of what hoggin' (or hawgin') for catfish is all about. While it flickered on the screen her husband's running commentary added further illumination.

In the first sequence, he and another man — presumably Luke — got out of a station wagon in that self-conscious way people have when they know they are being filmed. Then the camera swung around to provide an appreciation of the locale; a small lake or pond, surrounded by moss-hung, ancient trees — a scene right out of "I Was a Fugitive from a Georgia Chain Gang." Suddenly the picture blurred, due to a violent movement of the camera, after which the screen went black for some seconds.

"That's where old Clara dang near stepped on a water mocassin," my narrator said, trying without notable success to control his laughter. "Close to splittin' a gut, me and Luke was, watchin' her dance around."

"What happened to the snake?" I asked.

"Oh, we waited a while to enjoy it 'fore Luke shot the head off with his forty-five." He wiped a tear from one eye, then took a good belt of his bourbon.

The next sequence showed the two men wading out into the water, which soon reached to their waists.

"That's the secret," my host said. "You gotta know where them big, hollow cypresses is at. Just don't do to go gropin' around down there, blind-like."

In hoggin' (or hawgin'), you need at least two men. Having located a suitable underwater log, they move apart by ten to fifteen feet, taking up positions at the two extremities. First they have to reach down, chins trembling to remain above the water line, and hoist the big log to the surface. Then, while one holds a burlap bag over his end, the other pokes and prods and hollers, to chase anything that might be in the chute into flailing, frantic captivity at the other outlet. With luck, what comes rocketing out may be a ten, twenty, even forty-pound catfish, which the recipient will try to wrestle to the flat-bottomed punt floating nearby. If things go wrong, on the other hand, it could be . . . . but let's employ my host's words to describe that eventuality.

"You gotta remember to stay fifteen, maybe twenty, feet off-shore," he said, superimposing a comment.

"Why's that?" I asked, in the semi-darkness of his living room. His reply, when it came, revealed his surprise that anyone would ask such a stupid question.

"Why, on account of the snakes, of course," he said.

"A lot of them out there, I guess," I opined.

"Why, sure — water mocassins, cottonmouths, the odd coral snake. Real deadly, they is." He started to laugh again. "Never forget the moanin' Luke shut the bag on that big diamondback. Must have been six feet, easy. Figured Luke for dead, wrestlin' them coils. Funny enough to make you puke, I swear."

The film flickered on to its conclusion, the final shot of which was of the two men, smiling in somewhat embarrassed triumph, as they held up a string of a half-dozen big cats.

"Now, that was hoggin' (or hawgin')," my host declared. "Won't find nothin' finer."

"I guess it was, allright," I concurred, unable to think of anything further removed from casting for muskies on a northern lake at twilight, with a couple of loons, calling back and forth, beyond a nearby island. And how open, and wide, and non-claustrophobic it would be, come May, after the ice went out.

"Right glad you can spare the time to come in with us," he said.

"Don't figure the snakes will be as bad this spring," I suggested hopefully, the conjecture based on sheer cowardice.

He pondered that for a moment. "Not the rattlers," he said, "on account of the late season. They like it warm, you know what I mean. Cottonmouths, though, they should be just bustin' to fasten onto a leg or an arm."

I tried to imagine myself, standing in waist-deep, bayou water, groping down to find the end of a hollow cypress, so that I might eventually hope to wrestle a big catfish into submission. Or discard the writhing throws of a deadly water moccasin in the nick of time. It all seemed very ugly, very mean, nothing I wanted any part of, nothing to do with fishing, as I knew it. Just not any part of my heritage. The lights came back on.

"I really appreciate that," I said, as I drained the last of my drink, and got up to take my leave.

"Be showin' ya the real thing, come moanin'," he said. "Like to leave 'bout five, five-fifteen, me and Luke do. Snakes ain't stirrin' too much by then."

"I guess not," I said.

"Have bacon 'n eggs 'n grits ready, Clara will. Y'all be sure to come by, y' hear?"

"Mighty kind of you," I told him, "and I sure did appreciate seeing the film."

But I set my travelling alarm clock for three, sneaked out to my car upon awakening, and was a fur long piece down the road towards Texarcana, on the Texas border, before the sun edged up over the treetops.

Hoggin' or hawgin,' the entire Confederate Army couldn't have dragged me into that dismal swamp, to wrestle catfish in the turgid water, while cottonmouths and water mocassins and diamondbacks and coral snakes, and who the hell knew what else, took numbers to get their turns at me.

You had to remember not to get too close to shore, my host had said. That much, at least, made a lot of sense to me. By the time he and Luke rolled out of bed, rubbing their eyes and scratching, and Clara set the grits to cooking on the stove, I figured to be at least a hundred and fifty miles away, and still with my foot pushed down hard on the gas pedal.

I thought I might finally stop in Dallas for some lunch — at some place that didn't have catfish on the menu.

20.
A Day on Lake Onaman

As previously noted, the best part of many trips is in the planning. All too frequently getting there turns out to be half of not much fun. The mattresses in the hotel you've booked into are as hard and lumpy as old tumbling mats. Whoever is doing the cooking thinks that a good rule of thumb for steaks is thirty minutes per side. (It is, if you want to make shoes.) The river that looked so isolated and promising on the map turns out to be the site of the regional water skiing championships.

But earlier, pouring over brochures and compiling lists on a cold winter night, you can luxuriate in the conviction that *this* will be the one time when everything is perfect, when nothing can go wrong; the blue chip investment guaranteed to provide a pension of infinite memories to live off comfortably in your old age.

In fact, though, some of the really vintage fishing experiences are not planned at all, but just happen spontaneously, often when you least expect them. That's the way it was with the first day I spent on Lake Onaman.

A few years ago I found myself up in the Nipigon country, at the northwesternmost corner of Lake Superior, on the Trans-Canada highway. I had gone there in search of a novel, and had found it to be a much better one even than I had anticipated. What I haven't found yet is a way to write it.

Still, as I started back east, I was feeling that rare excitement, exhilirating yet enervating, that a writer experiences when he knows

142

that he has a story potentially great enough to permit him the luxury of being insecure about his ability to tell it truly and the way it deserves to be told. All the rest is a kind of running-on-the-spot.

It was an expansive interlude, a time for new experiences, for discovery, for dalliance, for intemperance. I love the stretch of the Trans-Canada that breasts Superior's austere, almost virginal north shore, but I had travelled it several times, including the current way west, a week earlier. So I decided to swing north on the old, narrower highway, No. 11, which would take me through Beardmore, Geraldton, Long Lac, Hearst, Kapuskasing and Cochrane, before beginning the long glide down into southern Ontario.

It was late afternoon when I left Nipigon. A couple of hours later the ragged hedge of jackpines along the horizon was starting to reach up for the sun, and I was beginning to wonder where I would spend the night; in that part of the country you don't find a Holiday Inn beckoning around every tenth turn of the road. Then I saw a motel sign and, obeying the arrow, turned off onto a gravel road. Set on the shore of a small, typically northern, wilderness lake, a hundred yards or so in from the highway, the setting was attractive enough but, as I pulled up to the office, I wasn't really expecting much beyond a hot shower, a tolerable meal, and a reasonably comfortable bed.

Inside, a man who I later came to know as the owner, glanced up from the portable typewriter he was hammering at with two fingers.

"Don't suppose I'll ever get used to this damn paper work," were his first words.

In his early forties, he was tall, thin, pleasant in an easy, matter-of-fact way — the kind of a man who would have been called 'Slim' on a western ranch. We exchanged the usual pleasantries, and then he took a key from one of the pegs on the board beside him and tossed it onto the counter.

"Should be comfortable in 17," he said.

"Fine, but don't you want me to sign in?" I asked.

He shrugged. "If you want. Me, I'd do it on the way to dinner. This time of day, a shower and a drink or two seem more important."

It was about then that I began to realize I'd stumbled onto something special. There are a couple of reasons why I'm not going to name the place, or pinpoint its location. First, I wouldn't want to run any risk of encouraging an invasion which might spoil a very good thing. And, realistically, it could have changed — including, God forbid, new management — since I was there last, which was a couple of years ago.

My room turned out to be a delightful surprise. Achieving a restful atmosphere through subdued lighting, decorated with sophisticated good taste, it was designed with the solicitous regard for creature comforts that you sometimes find in a superior big city hotel. Yet, far from being just a transplanted unit from a downtown Hilton, it somehow didn't intrude upon the wilderness, or lessen the awareness that there were loons out on the little lake beyond the window drapes, or moose chomping lily pads a quarter of a mile back in the bush.

I sandwiched a shower between a couple of drinks, then, ravenously hungry, went out to get dinner. The restaurant, also run by the motel owner, was back up the gravel road, across the highway. Constructed along square, utilitarian lines, it didn't look like much from the outside. At first glance, it didn't look like much from the inside, either — standard, formica-topped tables, red plastic catsup dispensers, plastic — covered chairs. But there was a small dining room to one side, with white table cloths, candles — and a liquor license — to which my expansive mood led me.

My waitress, a pleasant and efficient local girl, brought me a martini which was very dry, very generous, and very good. There was no formal menu, but she informed me that I could choose from roast beef, roast pork, braised short ribs, grilled whitefish, broiled lamb chops, a steak . . . or, if there was something else I particularly fancied, she'd see what the chef could do. Not wishing to push my luck unduly, I ordered the steak. When it came, it was about 14 ounces of magnificent sirloin, cooked to perfection, and served with a fine salad, fresh broccoli in a cheese sauce, and crisply browned, home fried potatoes.

When I asked for the check, after my third cup of coffee, she told me that it would simply be added onto my motel bill. Realizing queasily that she had never mentioned prices, I could imagine my tab running up to a total which would approximate the national debt of Paraguay. But a writer doesn't come upon a really great subject every week of his life so I pushed all thoughts of settlement from my cowardly, unprotesting mind.

On the way back, I stopped by the motel office to complete the formalities of checking-in. The proprietor was cleaning and oiling a reel. Behind him on the wall there were four or five mounted fish, including a walleye that I guessed would go close to twelve pounds. After I had signed in, we talked fishing for a while — a nice, relaxed conversation. He told me that they operated three fly-in camps to the north.

"You going to get a chance to wet a line while you're here?" he asked.

I told him that I had brought along my tackle, but so far hadn't taken it out of the trunk of the car.

"Be glad to fly you in for a day," he suggested. "What do you like to fish for?"

I told him that some walleyes for the frying pan and a few big Northern Pike would do just fine, and alomst before I had time to think about it, arrangements had been made for me to take off after breakfast the next morning. It wasn't that he used high pressure methods; just that the idea evolved so naturally, almost inevitably, from the situation and the mood. Again, price wasn't mentioned, nor did I bring up the subject. I might be digging myself in deeper and deeper, but the hell with it; my conscience could scold me some bleak, rainy November afternoon back in Toronto.

"Onaman should do the trick," my host told me. "Have you in there in about thirty minutes flying time. Pick you up at No. 2 camp around five. Couple of drinks and dinner here, and you can still make a hundred miles on the way back before your head hits the pillow."

I slept like a saint that night, in the heat-controlled comfort of my room, and ten hours later, after bacon and eggs and home-made English muffins and jam and coffee, I walked down to the dock behind the motel office with my fishing rod and tackle box. It was not what you would call a Chamber of Commerce morning; there was a lot of low-scudding black clouds, and the heavy, humid air was thick with a kind of half-rain, half-mist. More like late October than early September, and you could just see the far, hazy margin of the small lake.

The float-plane was a black Otter, with orange markings, which had obviously logged a lot of air miles. The pilot, on the other hand, looked to be about twenty years old, and I hoped that he had learned a lot about bush flying in a short time. There were two other passengers — a couple of aging, hung-over, pulp and paper camp cooks, heading "back in" after a few days of drinking up their accumulated pay in the beer parlours of the district.

We took off into the gloom, the pontoons just managing to squeeze over the spires of the jackpines at the far end of the lake. A few minutes later the sun broke through, and we were flying over a seemingly infinite expanse of lakes, rivers, deltas, rock outcroppings and moose meadows. Once the ribbon of the highway had slid away from us, we saw no signs of civiliation for forty or fifty miles. When it came into view, Lake Onaman was much larger than I had expected, about the size of one of the larger of the Kawarthas. We banked quite steeply over one end to come up into the wind, and, as we were swinging over the shore line, the young pilot turned back and pointed down through his side window. I looked in that direction and saw a group of thirty or forty large animals running across a rocky clearing. Not knowing what they were, I glanced inquiringly at one of the cooks. He shouted that they were woodland caribou, one of the few surviving herds in that part of the country.

A few minutes later we taxied up to a crude, though sturdily-biult dock, to which were tied a half-dozen outboard motor boats. The pilot let me out, with a shouted reminder that he would look for me at camp No. 2 around five, then closed the door, revved up his motor, and headed out into the lake to take off again with the two camp cooks.

By then a tall, powerful-looking man of about thirty, with the fiery red beard of a Norse discoverer, and the build of an NFL defensive end, had ambled down to greet me. Launderer, mechanic, cook, bartender, resident woodland expert and philosopher, Charlie was in charge of the base camp on Onaman. In the summer season, just drawing to a close, he had to look after well-heeled guests from Toronto, Detroit, Chicago, Cleveland, and other, more far-flung metropoli. Playing himself, he was a lover of peace and quiet, a quite hopeless poet, and a casual, sometime, post-graduate student in oceanography at Dalhousie University.

Located in a flat, low clearing, the main building had originally been constructed as a bunkhouse by a long since departed lumbering operation. Crudely built, weathered by many years of summer suns and winter blizzards, it had been remodeled to include a bar and recreation room (with stone fireplace), and eight or ten rooms for guests.

Charlie and I had coffee at a table in the dining room, the walls of which were completely covered with pictures from *Playboy*, *Penthouse* and similar magazines. The radio-telephone hookup between Onaman and the motel had informed him of my coming, and my lunch, including a couple of cans of beer, had been placed in the outboard motor boat assigned to me. Charlie gave me a map of Onaman, on which he had noted some of the best fishing stretches, and pinpointed the location of Camp No. 2. on an island at the eastern end of the lake, where the Otter would pick me up towards the end of the afternoon.

By about 10:30 that morning I was trolling around the rocky points, and along the weed-encircled bays of Lake Onaman. The fishing was fantastic; there was almost always a walleye on almost as soon as the line had a chance to trail straight-out behind the boat, and you could count on being tied to a really good Northern Pike, some in the twelve to fifteen pound range, about every half-hour or so. I didn't keep any of the fish, of course, but it was an awful lot of fun.

I ate my lunch on mainland point — baloney sandwiches, a tomato, a couple of hard-boiled eggs, pickles, homemade bran muffins, a beer, a thermos of coffee. The sun was out then, and it was drowsily warm, and there was no sign of fall around the perimeter of the lake, apart from a single, prematurely-yellow branch on a poplar on the far shore.

During the afternoon the fishing slackened off a little, but it was still so ridicously easy to catch pickerel that I lost interest after a while, and spent most of the time just exploring the shoreline, with the rod lying in the bottom of the boat. Occasionally I would try a few casts, just for a change of pace, and on one of those I lost a really fine Northern Pike. I think it might have gone twenty-five pounds or better, but I never got a chance to inspect him at close range because he came hurtling up out of the water, shaking his head like a marlin, and threw the hooks on his first, savage run.

It was an idyllic few hours on that big, unspoiled, hauntingly-lonely lake. Apart from the low, throttled-back drone of my motor, there were sights or sounds that you mightn't have seen or heard a thousand, ten thousand, years before — no rumble of traffic from any nearby highway, no jet trails across the sky, no shouts of water skiers. I watched, drifting, as a family of otters played around a moss-covered, rocky point. I surprised a big old beaver working on the dome of the house it was building against the winter that would all too soon begin to creep over the land. I stared down a big bull moose at the foot of a small bay, followed it with my eyes as it lumbered awkwardly away, crashing through the underbrush, into the deep woods. Towards the end of the afternoon I kept three walleyes, thinking that I would somehow find a way to clean and cook them later that evening, after I was picked up and flown back to the motel.

Thw weather closed in so suddenly that there was virtually no warning. One moment the lake was sparkling under the warm sun; the next, clouds so low that they seemed to envelope the treetops, were spreading across the sky, trailing rain and mist which quickly blotted out the far shoreline, and caused the temperature to drop ten or fifteen degrees in as many minutes. By then it was about four o'clock, and I stood every prospect of ending the day very wet and chilled to the bone.

According to the map Charlie had given me, Camp No. 2 was on one of a group of islands a half-mile or so ahead. I turned the 10 h.p. motor up as high as it would go and made a run for it, head down, crouched low against the drifting, chill rain. Ten minutes later I drifted in alongside the makeshift dock, jumped out, tied the boat hurriedly, and scampered over the rocks into the welcome shelter of the tent.

It was a well-constructed, if temporary, canvas refuge, tall enough to let you move around in comfort, and with a wood floor. My most immediate need was to cast off the damp and chill of the run down the lake in the rain. I found a Coleman gasoline stove and lit it. Next I filled a kettle from a pail of water and put it on to boil. Then I took time to loom around. Though rustic, the tent camp was very small, and comfortably equipped and furnished. There was a small table and two benches; a double-decker bunk with sheets and blankets; a small, gas-operated refrigerator; filled lamps; pots and pans; a can opener; cups and plates; knives, forks, and spoons. The larder, in a copper-lined cupboard under the stove, offered a wide variety of canned and freeze-dried foods, plus all the requisite staples — powdered orange juice, instant coffee, tea bags, tinned milk, soups, sugar, salt, pepper, garlic powder, lamb stew, liver and onions, dried mushrooms, dehydrated apples and pears, jam, marmalade, chicken a la king, even a couple of foiled-wrapped, ready-to-reconstitute, T-bone steaks. A cardboard carton held a dozen or so cans of beer. A 'library'

148

of sorts, too — a couple of dozen paperbacks in a fruit basket in one corner.

I lit one of the lamps against the gloom, and sat down at the table to drink my coffee. Outside the rain continued and the wind was rising, but it was warm and comfortable in the tent. By then I was sure that the plane would not be returning for me that day — not with the clouds right down on the deck and the promise of a very early twilight. That was fine with me; I had no schedule to maintain, and the prospect of spending the night in my snug, well-stocked shelter was by no means unattractive.

Then, as abruptly as it had closed over the lake, the dirty weather relinquished its hold. The rain stopped, and the sun came out, lower now towards the horizon. I went to the triangular entrance, and threw the canvas flap to one side. Moisture dripped from the trees, the air was incredibly clear, and the whole world semmed newly washed.

About ten minutes later I heard the drone of the Otter, and just had time to empty the coffee pot and wash my cup before it came taxiing into the dock.

A half-hour after that I was taking a shower in my room back at the motel. That was a two martini, shrimp cocktail, onion soup and rare roast beef evening at the restaurant up on the highway.

It was almost dark when I went to the office to check out. The moment of truth was at hand. I had had my fling, crowded an awful lot of good living into the past twenty-four hours, and now it was time to pay the piper. I cringed to think what his fee, all mention of which had been politely avoided until then, would prove to be.

My host sat at his desk to make up the bill, while I leaned on the counter. He asked me about my day in at Onaman, and I told him I had enjoyed every minute of it.

"Didn't think we were going to get you out of there for a while," he said, writing down figures.

"That wouldn't have been any great hardship."

"No, I guess not," he said, coming over to the counter. "Well here's the damage."

I glanced at the bill. The bottom line showed a total of sixty-one dollars. My expression must have reflected my bewilderment.

"Problems? Maybe I added something wrong."

"No, no — it's just that this can't be everything."

"Think so. Don't believe I forgot anything."

I couldn't believe it — the room, the fine meals, the plane, the use of the boat in at Onaman, the packed lunch . . . .

"But you can't make any money at this rate," I told him.

"Well, I gave you a break, maybe, on the Otter. Frank had to go right by there anyway, though, with those two cooks."

"Okay, but it just doesn't seem enough." Maybe, I thought, I'll go down in history after all: the first writer in all the ages of man to argue that a bill was too low.

"You drive in here in a Lincoln Continental, I guarantee you it'll be different," he said, with a twinkle in his eye. "Anyway, maybe we'll lean on you a little harder the next time."

"Well, you can believe there'll be a next time," I told him.

And there was — a next, and a next, and a next. Every trip in to Onaman has been great, but none better than the first time. Come to think of it, I'm due for another return visit. Maybe, now that I've finished this book . . . .

No advance planning, though.